Trauma Demystified
Students and Practitioners

Trauma Demystified: A Guide for Students and Practitioners

Divine Charura, Mark McFetridge and Emma Bradshaw

Open University Press

Open University Press
McGraw Hill
Unit 4
Foundation Park
Roxborough Way
Maidenhead
SL6 3UD

Email: emea_uk_ireland@mheducation.com
World wide web: www.mheducation.co.uk

Commissioning Editor: Hannah Church
Editorial Assistant: Phoebe Hills
Content Product Manager: Graham Jones

British Library Cataloguing in Publication Data
A catalogue record of this book is available from the British Library

ISBN-13: 978-0-33-525174-2
ISBN-10: 0-33-525174-9
eISBN: 978-0-33-525175-9

Typeset by Transforma Pvt. Ltd., Chennai, India

Praise for this book

"Trauma Demystified is an indispensable guide for anyone seeking to understand and heal from trauma. Charura, McFetridge, and Bradshaw blend cutting-edge research with compassionate insights, making complex concepts accessible. Their holistic approach and practical tools empower readers to navigate the path to inner healing. A must-read for both professionals and those affected by trauma."
Professor Nahid Nasrat, Department of Psychology at
The Chicago School, US

"Much is written about trauma, but much less is written with such a depth of practice experience, academic insight and an honouring of the human experience. Charura, McFetridge and Bradshaw have, in this wonderful text, brought together so much that is helpful to all those involved in working with trauma. An essential text that takes our understanding to a new level."
Professor Andrew Reeves, Professor of Counselling Professions and
Mental Health, University of Chester, UK

"Trauma Demystified is a comprehensive approach to trauma. The book explores different facets of trauma, bringing together numerous perspectives in one volume. The authors' knowledge and expertise on trauma are evident throughout the book. Unlike other books focusing on trauma – the authors' humanity and personhood shine through from beginning to end. The book's strength lies in centring of the human experience, of relationship, of learning from grandparents, of the importance of remembering that trauma experiences are idiosyncratic, encouraging the reader to reflect on their understanding and knowledge of trauma and human distress while holding ethical considerations in mind. This book will be of immensurable value to counselling and psychotherapy students and qualified therapists alike."
Lesley Dougan, Programme Lead, MA Counselling & Psychotherapy
Practice, Liverpool John Moores University, UK

"Accessible can sometimes be overused when describing an introductory academic text but it is truly applicable to this very readable guide to trauma for the practitioner. Written with compassion and humour, it manages to provide an excellent overview combining summaries of academic research with narratives about people – the authors share their own experiences alongside illustrative material based on their many years of experience. It is up to date, containing welcome references to moral injury and the importance of culture and spirituality,

for example. Alongside best practice sifted from the literature it also contains a good deal of wisdom, making it ideal for those wanting to know more about our current understanding of trauma and how to help those impacted by it."

Professor Gary Latchford, Joint Programme Director, Clinical Psychology Training Programme, University of Leeds, UK

Contents

Acknowledgements

We would like to thank all our family members, friends and colleagues for continually supporting us during the process of writing this book. We feel immensely privileged to have worked with so many people who have had the courage to share their experiences and aspects of their lives, often during very difficult times following trauma. Being facilitators of learning within universities and other educational settings where psychologists and other mental health professionals train, we are thankful to students and colleagues whose curiosity has highlighted to us the importance of demystifying trauma and hence encouraging us to write this book.

List of acronyms

ACE	adverse childhood experience
ACT	acceptance and commitment therapy
APA	American Psychological Association
ASD	autism spectrum disorder
CBT	Cognitive Behavioural Therapy
CBT-T	cognitive behavioural therapy for trauma
CFT	compassion focused therapy
CPT	cognitive processing therapy
CPTSD	complex PTSD
CT	cognitive therapy
DBT	dialectical behavioural therapy
DSM-III	*The Diagnostic and Statistical Manual of Mental Disorders*, 3rd edition
DSM-5	*The Diagnostic and Statistical Manual of Mental Disorder*, 5th edition
DSM-5 TR	*The Diagnostic and Statistical Manual of Mental Disorders*, 5th edition: text revision (2022)
DSO	disturbances in self-organisation
ECT	Electroconvulsive Therapy
EMDR	eye movement desensitisation and reprocessing
FSS	functional somatic syndromes
ICD-11	International Classification of Diseases, 11th revision
NET	narrative exposure therapy
NHS	National Health Service
NICE	National Institute for Health and Care Excellence.
OTSR	ongoing traumatic stress response
PDM-2	*Psychodynamic Diagnostic Manual*, 2nd edition: PDM-2
PCT	present centred therapy
PDT	psychodynamic therapy
PE	prolonged exposure
PTGI	Post-Traumatic Growth Inventory
PTMF	power threat meaning framework
PTSD	post-traumatic stress disorder
RCT	randomised controlled trial
TC	therapeutic community
tf-CBT	trauma-focused CBT
TIC	Trauma-informed Care

1 Introduction

Overview

- This chapter will outline the aims of this book. In addition, we will begin to highlight the contemporary and contentious perspectives around trauma.
- This will include what is commonly understood about the complexity of working with trauma as well as exploring gaps in knowledge.
- A unique aspect of this chapter will be its capacity to stimulate thought and challenge assumptions about trauma to illuminate an alternative perspective.

In writing this book, we approached colleagues, clients and trainees in dialogue to enquire about what they may want to be included in a book such as this. Furthermore, we have also drawn from numerous recommendations of research and identified priorities for clinical practice in working with those presenting with trauma experiences.

Here we begin by highlighting the contentious and contemporary issues in relation to trauma. Several meta-analyses and systematic literature reviews have demonstrated that a number of psychological therapies are effective for trauma and that there's evidence for an array of modalities and approaches. This has led us to argue that part of what is both contemporary and contentious, is the drive for specific treatments for 'psychological disorders' including PTSD. Thus, the therapy field at the moment is at a paradigm shift where practitioners need to be open and flexible when working with trauma. We should be able to think about what works for whom and acknowledge that what does work will vary from individual to individual. This approach includes all of the combinations of holistic and trauma-focused therapies as well as valuing the bio-psycho-social-sexual-spiritual-cultural aspects of recovery. Furthermore, this includes a greater appreciation of what has come to be termed *moral injury* which relates to acting in a way that goes against one's values or witnessing events that result in a loss of trust and faith. There has also been an explosion of contemporary ways of conceptualising trauma focused on the way in which people experience this within their bodies (embodied trauma).

Introducing the authors

Personal reflection: Divine

I (Divine) started working in mental health settings in the late 1990s. I remember being a university student on various mental health placements in different psychiatric asylum hospitals in Leeds (northern England, UK). These included hospitals which have now been closed, such as St. James Hospital psychiatric Roundhay Wing, and High Royds Hospital which was one of the oldest asylums in the UK. Opened in 1888 as the West Riding Pauper Lunatic Asylum, High Royds Hospital was where in 2002 I first became interested in working with trauma.

At the time being a student on what was then termed psychiatric placements, I spent most of my shift hours in different inpatient units, supporting patients who were detained under the UK mental health act. The Mental Health Act (1983), updated in 2007, is the main legislation that covers the psychiatric assessment, treatment and rights of individuals presenting with mental ill health. Many of these patients were heavily sedated with medication and many times I was on duty to escorted patients to the Electroconvulsive Therapy (ECT) suite, where patients were subjected as part of their treatment to Electroconvulsive Therapy. I remember saying in clinical supervision to two colleagues, one of whom was a psychiatrist and the other a psychologist, how uncomfortable I felt with the clinical approach I was witnessing. This included restraining or injecting 'patients' who were severely unwell and then secluding and monitoring them through a small window of what was called a seclusion/de-escalation room. I felt deeply challenged by the impact this was having on me as well as those I witnessed experiencing this. These experiences made me question the therapeutic value of these services. I soon decided that I would shift my focus and continuing development to further training as a psychotherapist and psychologist who would contribute to a different therapeutic approach. It was evident to me that nearly all the patients I was meeting and who were admitted in the intensive care psychiatric units' psychiatric wards, or the psychotherapy settings I later worked in, had all had traumatic life experiences. These experiences, whether in childhood or later in their life, had then contributed to their psychological distress.

In my experience, however, sadly many of these patients were given diagnoses and labels that did not always evidence clinicians' acknowledgement of the aetiology of the individuals' psychological distress and presentation as a trauma response. Thankfully, the 'psychiatric asylums' in the UK are now shut down, and my work over the last two decades has included working in the UK National Health Service (NHS) in psychotherapy and psychology services in which I have witnessed how staff attitudes and services are changing for the better.

As a professor of counselling psychology at York St John University I feel privileged to be now contributing in facilitating the training of psychologists and I champion trauma-informed understanding to psychological distress. Furthermore, my specialist area of interest is in understanding the impact of trauma and the ways in which we all can enhance mental wellbeing across the lifespan. I also work as a practitioner psychologist, coaching psychologist and psychotherapist in private practice.

Having been trained in the humanistic, systemic, psychodynamic and cognitive behavioural modalities, I have come to appreciate that they all help me and the clients/patients I work with, and are a variety of ways of understanding the process of psychological maladjustment that ensues after traumatic experiences. Following my own life experiences, and working with those presenting with trauma in different contexts, I have arrived at the point of co-writing this book which aims to demystify trauma.

Personal reflection: Mark

I may have been destined to be a clinical psychologist from the age of 12 when I, sadly, became precociously over-skilled at emotionally and physically supporting my mother with terminal cancer. I had, up to then, experienced a loving and nurturing childhood from my unusually older parents (for the 1960s and '70s). When my mother, Rose, died a year later, I recall my decision (and exactly where I was) that I would 'cure cancer', so nobody would have to go through this again.

We all know I didn't succeed in the medical aspiration of this vow, but I did develop my capacity over the coming years to alleviate the post-traumatic distress experienced by people following overwhelming circumstances. If this wasn't enough to secure my future trajectory, my father had been injured in the Second World War and, like many returning soldiers, did not talk about the war. This influential parental combination therefore sealed my fate as a (second generation) trauma expert. I couldn't have chosen more wisely if it had been conscious!

However, to follow my path as a clinical psychologist and future traumatologist, I had to turn away from my alternative (fantasy) career as a rock drummer to rival Phil Collins of Genesis in the 1980s. Perhaps Phil would have made a great psychologist if he had had my childhood; there but for the grace of (the rock) God go I?

Building on my curious teenage psychological interests in hypnosis and dreams, I managed to stay awake for just enough of my Psychology A-level to pass reasonably well. I could then go on to be a little more alert, if more distracted, and gain a Psychology degree, and then seek whatever clinical experiences I could as steps toward clinical Psychology training.

Qualifying in 1987, I took up my first post in a very deprived area of West Yorkshire (UK), previously known for its 'Shoddy & Mungo' – the industrial byproducts of the more lucrative woollen trade in nearby Leeds. I was shocked to learn, as I started out in 1987, that 50 per cent of women from this area had died in childbirth a century earlier. In many ways the local mental health care had not advanced a great deal in recent years, but I had been drawn to the new inspirational practitioner psychologists that I knew I could learn from. At the same time, there was a national campaign started by the prime-time TV presenter and journalist Esther Rantzen to commission a telephone support service and charity named Childline. Starting as a story about the prevalence of current child sexual abuse in the UK, this cascaded into our mental health services as we started to have open conversations with our clients about whether anything similar had ever happened to them.

Just as was the case after the Second World War, when the numbers of the traumatised outstripped resources, we as a psychology and mental health service, (once again) discovered groups. Judith Herman went on to note in her 1992 classic *Trauma and Recovery* that our history is littered with the repeated forgetting and rediscovering of trauma. I had to learn much from my colleagues and our clients, and quickly. I am glad now I took the opportunity to linger a little longer, but after seven years I felt the need to move elsewhere. I actually felt this itch sooner, but fortunately realised in time that this was for no better reason than the pattern of my recent career (moving on every two years, or less). Staying longer in this service lead to me gaining the experience of working with the same clients for five years in some cases, and coming to appreciate the true extent of some peoples' past (and sometimes ongoing) horrors. Significant moments included supporting a courageous young mother to confront her abuser in the presence of his ecclesiastical colleagues, and then my facilitating his transfer to a therapeutic service for sex offenders. She had, of course, been far from his only victim, and was not able to disclose this within the first two years of therapy due to silence inducing self-blame and his concurrent coercive influence.

Other memorable clients helped me to learn to negotiate, and equally prioritise, my own safety in therapy. The treasured Special Forces knife had to go in a locked office drawer if another client and I were to work on her past trauma. I (in fact, we) could not risk me being re-experienced as someone from her traumatic past with this knife to hand. It did go in the drawer; we did do the work together; and I am here to tell the story and remember her fondly.

I did move on geographically and professionally, but within weeks trauma and human exploitation reacquainted itself with me (and this was at the seaside too!). Happy times in my new teams started to turn sour as a client disclosed a current sexual relationship with a consultant psychiatrist. I vividly remember her exclamation: 'Who is going to believe me? I'm a psychiatric patient and he has written books on female sexual problems.' I believed her, and so did the judge, and he went to prison. Although she had her own reasons for not wanting to go through the complaint process, she had not been his only victim. Even more shockingly, he had not been the only perpetrator in the local mental health services; I found myself giving testimony 11 years later about the experience of trying to raise alarm and action (pre-safeguarding) to the Kerr Haslam NHS Inquiry in 2005. The theme and central question of this inquiry would sadly echo the Saville inquiry of 2014 (Jimmy Saville, OBE): how come this abuse was such a well-known secret? I was learning that the probable answer was that the system around the victims is also 'groomed'. In the case of Saville, this might be considered to be the entire UK, with the exception of his victims.

I did some more everyday things in this new post too, and loved it; being part of two community mental health teams for a day each per week was welcome respite. However, like the experience of my co-authors, once you recognise trauma, it keeps knocking at your door. Rather than pretending I wasn't in, I decided to embrace this, and take on a doctoral research project into the process and outcome of a new 'fringe' trauma therapy called EMDR (which I frankly thought was a bit wacky and unnecessary at the time, in 1998).

So that critics couldn't call me biased, I went off to New York in 1998 to be trained by Francine Shapiro. I was stunned to later find how effective this new approach had been with my participants, all drawn from the local NHS waiting list suffering from long-standing PTSD. It seemed that it may be a good idea to carry on using EMDR where appropriate, alongside my old therapeutic favourite – the group.

My third clinical, and now consultant, post facilitated this fantastically and threw me into the world of therapeutic communities (TCs). Here I really learned the therapeutic power of peer support, compassionate challenge and friendship; my role was to simply facilitate this, and (like EMDR) then get out of the way. My 22 years at the Retreat, York showed how a supportive and containing managerial system around a highly reflective, kindly team can achieve astounding clinical change. I am saddened that this has passed (all things indeed do!), but more so that it may well be some time before this formula can be rediscovered within our current beleaguered mental health services and NHS.

There is however a current groundswell of interest and enthusiasm for Trauma-informed Care (TIC); my co-authors and I hope to contribute to this community of ideas by laying down some of our knowledge of trauma and traumatic experiences from our clinical and research careers. We hope this may act as a catalyst for you and your colleagues in the special contributions you will make.

Personal reflection: Emma

I feel privileged to have engaged in this writing project with my colleagues Divine and Mark. We have had many interesting discussions about the nature of trauma which have highlighted the complexity of this subject: something that we hope to share with you in this book. My first experience of helping people who have experienced trauma was when I volunteered with the Samaritans while studying for a degree in psychology. I spent many a night shift speaking on the phone with people who were suffering the effects of trauma which felt unbearable to them in that moment. I was struck by how restorative it could be for someone to connect with another human being while in a moment of deep emotional pain. That experience led to my realisation that I wanted to become a counselling psychologist and to develop my therapeutic skills in this field.

My understanding of the effects of trauma and how healing can occur has developed (and continues to develop) since then. While I have trained in the psychodynamic, CBT, CFT, ACT and DBT models, my approach is humanistic, and the therapeutic relationship remains at the core of the work I do.

Working in an alcohol addiction service led to my understanding of coping mechanisms linked to living with the effects of trauma (e.g., by drinking alcohol). I further realised that the opportunity to speak about traumatic life experiences within the frame of a containing therapeutic relationship often promotes a movement towards positive change.

While working in a chronic pain service I learnt about the complex interaction between mind and body resulting from trauma. At that stage, I trained in EMDR and began to witness the transformational effects of this therapy: that healing trauma can bring about a reduction of suffering for both mind and body. Since then I am honoured to have worked therapeutically with people using EMDR in both private and NHS outpatient services.

My work in an inpatient service at The Retreat, York was another influential experience for me. I enjoyed connecting with the women on the unit who were trying hard to function in life after experiencing trauma in childhood. I developed a deeper understanding of the ongoing effects of attachment difficulties, neglect and abuse in childhood and how this is often misunderstood in our society.

In recent years I have taught on the Doctorate in Counselling Psychology at York St John University. It is a pleasure to contribute to the educational journey of trainees who are working extremely hard in their bid to help others. I now work mainly in independent practice, offering therapy to adults who wish to process past trauma and move forward in a positive way. These experiences have led me to contribute to this book, which I hope will encourage a trauma-informed approach to mental healthcare.

About this book

Welcome to this book, in which you will be introduced to contemporary understanding of trauma and the trauma-informed approaches. At the heart of this book is our commitment to demystifying trauma through giving examples of vignettes which relay trauma-informed formulations of therapeutic relationships we have engaged in over the last few decades.

This book aims to meet a few objectives. First, it aims to demystify the principles and theory as written in trauma texts. Secondly, this book aims to offer clear definitions of terms and concepts of trauma and trauma therapy. To inform this book, we enquired of a range of students and trainee psychologists about the areas of trauma that they were mystified by. We also engaged with many qualified therapists of a wide range of modalities including psychodynamic, cognitive behavioural, existential-humanistic, and integrative about the knowledge informing their practice.

Thirdly, we also draw from psychosocial and transcultural perspectives. These highlight that trauma is more than an intrapsychic process (residing in the person) but rather a relational experience embedded in relational and systemic processes. Thus, the relational aspect is always relevant, even though it may not have been the source of the traumatic experience. We therefore assert that healing is facilitated within relationships, including the therapeutic relationship.

This book draws on psychological research and theory and offers examples that enable trainees, clinicians and other readers an opportunity to reflect on their knowledge and practice.

To make the book accessible, our intention was to write it in a style that we hope is equally engaging and academic. This was done by reflecting where relevant on fictional case vignettes we created. However, in creating these vignettes we drew upon many decades of experience of our clinical work with individuals presenting with trauma. The fictional vignettes are therefore an amalgamation of lived experiences and aspects of identity (i.e. names, gender, age, relationship status) and do not represent any individual or their experience. They therefore are fictional cases created for reflection purposes only and do not bear any correlation to specific clients we have known or worked with.

The central aim of the book is to reflect on the centrality of the therapeutic relationship in working with trauma, at both the individual and systemic levels. We conclude by considering possible future steps and direction in all our shared working with trauma.

Terms, concepts and respect for difference and diversity

For the purposes of this book, the terms therapist, clinician and practitioner or practitioner psychologist are used interchangeably. These terms cover a range of professionals working with trauma. This includes practitioners whose primary role is therapeutic, for example psychologists, counsellors, psychotherapists, psychological therapists and to some extent psychiatrists or health professionals in a wide range of contexts who work with those who present with or have experienced trauma.

In some trauma research studies and trauma therapeutic practice, the terms *'patient'*, *'service user'*, *'client'* may be used. In this book the authors prefer to use the term *'client'* in the main unless there is specific reason not to do so. For example, in line with acknowledging the importance of diversity, where we refer to the terms *'patient' or 'service user'*, this is in the spirit of respect for the diverse practice contexts where these terms may be used or even preferred by those being supported in these services.

We offer the chapters that follow in the spirit of continual reflecting and learning together. This is towards our shared aim of advancing our understanding and research approaches and knowledge in ways that are inclusive. In demystifying trauma, we hope to facilitate an accessible way for you to continue to learn about trauma and for this book to be the platform from which you can explore beyond.

2 Historical context: on learning from our grandparents (as they have gone before us)

Mark McFetridge, Divine Charura and Emma Bradshaw

Overview

- This chapter considers what the authors have learned from, and how they were influenced by, the experiences of their grandparents and parents.
- We highlight the power of sharing accounts (or 'stories') of experiences with others, for both parties.
- We explore potential facilitative conditions for therapeutic trauma work with our clients, including attention to spiritual and transpersonal aspects.

Different stories

Whether we had the opportunity to know them or not, we have all had grandparents and they had lives that have influenced ours. We (authors) enjoyed thinking together of what we knew of our grandparents' experience-rich lives, and what we might learn from these stories that could both assist our understanding of trauma and our therapeutic endeavours.

We hope the following accounts provide some historical and personal context for you when considering the range of therapeutic and theoretical issues that emerged from our shared reflections.

Shaving in the dark

My (MM) grandfather Charles, like many 15-year-old boys of his day, went off to join the First World War in Northern France, 1914–1918, and miraculously survived (unlike many).

Figure 2.1 Grandma Rosemary, Grandad Charles and Grandson Mark

I recall visiting him in his older age and discovering him shaving in the dark. As a young aspiring practitioner psychologist, I worried this was a sign of his obvious confusion and insidious cognitive decline. With an unintended but still patronising tone, I gently asked why he was doing this (at least I had the sense to ask).

Grandad Charles laughed heartily, and explained he was quite happy shaving in the dark, just as he had safely practised ever since returning from the muddy trenches of the Great War. He explained that in 1915 if you didn't shave in the dark, you would lose more than a whisker to an alerted sniper, and it would probably be the last close shave you would ever have. I realised the irony; if Grandad hadn't learned to shave in the dark, I probably wouldn't be here to receive illuminating answers to my patronising questions.

Pennies make pounds

Charles returned from the war to his home city in northern England, and he was fortunate (for me, too) soon to meet my grandmother Rosemary. She had been an Irish immigrant as a 7-year-old girl in the early years of the twentieth century. It is shocking for us to now consider that until the 1950s, landlords in the UK were apparently able to legally display signs stating: *No dogs, no blacks, no Irish*.

Rosemary and Charles were both part of the Roman Catholic faith and community, a crucial element to them gaining permission to marry at that time but, I suspect, of more fundamental importance to Rosemary than Charles. I spent time with my grandparents in my teenage years and learned the story of my grandmother working as a cleaner in multiple simultaneous jobs and saving every penny she could; a family saying she often quoted was *'pennies make pounds'*. Rosemary was able to save sufficient pennies to buy their own terraced house, a real achievement, and an unusual life choice among the working-class of their northern city in the early 1900s (but then perhaps not, given the landlords' discriminatory signs?).

The street on which the house was sited was later subject to a compulsory purchase to make way for new university buildings. I wondered if it had knowingly been sold to Rosemary at a 'knockdown' price by the previous owner, knowing but not disclosing its inevitable future? However, the university, in return for the compulsory purchase, granted a large semi-detached house rent-free for as long as they both lived. This proved a sound arrangement of a further 70 years for this prudent young couple. After my grandmother Rosemary died, Charles (at the age of 87 years) started smoking and visiting the local betting shop to gamble on the horse races. Once again, but now as an almost experienced practitioner psychologist, I expressed my patronising concern. I asked Grandad Charles what his doctors thought of him now smoking? Charles laughed heartily and reminded me that his doctors were all dead.

Charles enjoyed a further three lively (if lonelier) years to just before his ninetieth birthday. By the time both my grandparents had died no such discriminatory and offensive signs were permitted to be displayed by landlords; however, primetime UK terrestrial television was still laughing at the prospect of having a Black family next door, as presumably were the audience (*Love thy Neighbour*; see *Key resources and further reading*).

The colonisation of the African people

One of us (DC) had the privilege to hear a first-hand account of the arrival of white visitors to Southern Africa. Great Grandma Nana T was 100 years old when I was aged 7, and she told me how she had witnessed the colonisation of the African people. At the time she referred to how many native African people, during her era, didn't wear clothes. She described, as a young girl, experiencing the confusion and pain of she and her fellow tribe being different from the white settlers.

Before they knew it, she went from a sense of freedom within her family, to being placed (detained) in what were termed 'Reserves', in which Black families now had to remain and work. She spoke to me about the history of slavery in my family in some detail. As I was very young, I didn't understand everything she was saying to me, but I can now appreciate the traumatic nature of her experience. Nana T was perhaps also experiencing the transgenerational traumatic effect of slavery that she was processing through African oral archaeology – passing the narrative down to me, one of her great-grandchildren, so I would understand difference, diversity, trauma and the effects of transgenerational trauma.

A generation later, my paternal Grandma spoke to me about being a young woman and witnessing people being killed in what they called *the liberation struggle* (1964 to 1979). She spoke a great deal about her older brother, and others she knew, who had returned from the conflict, but were never the same afterwards. The cultural perspective and understanding were that these family members and friends had done *bad things* and may have witnessed the killing of other human beings during the liberation struggle, and therefore they had become 'possessed' and 'mad'. This was an interesting cultural way of (very likely) conceptualising the symptoms of PTSD and the chronic effects of over-whelming traumatic experience.

It's just what happened, and that's that!

When I (EB) think about my family and some of the potentially traumatic experiences I've heard them refer to, they weren't posed as traumatic, but instead were normalised as this is just that what happened. My grandma was an only child, as her mother had been the oldest of nine children and had to look after her siblings most of her life as a young person. She therefore decided that she just wanted one child, who was my gran. My great grandparents were in their late thirties when he was called up for service in the First World War (1914–1918). My gran had a memory of being a young girl the night before her father went to war; they just huddled together, staying awake all night hugging because they didn't know whether he was going to come back or not. It is now evident to me that the fear, and helplessness she experienced, and the memory of that night, stayed with her throughout her life. However, it wasn't presented as traumatic by her, but rather as just something difficult that happened, without any lasting effect. On the paternal side of my family, my dad (now in his eighties) was also an only child. Dad was born in 1940 and, during the war, his father had been a Major in the Royal Engineers and was posted to India. In the post-war period he worked for an oil company in Persia (now Iran). My dad was similarly 'posted', at the age of 8 years, to a boarding school in the UK. He has told me that he recalls being upset on his first night as a boarder, before accepting his fate and 'getting on with it'. He made friends with the other boys and they found contentment by starting a model-making club in the basement, an activity that he still enjoys today. It really struck me how my father learned, because of this experience at such a young age, to find a way to cope with his difficult emotions.

When my grandmother went to visit her husband in Persia for a year they rented out their house, and whoever leased it accepted the condition that they looked after their son during his school holidays. My dad told me he had enjoyable holidays with a lovely family, but nonetheless he went for a whole year without seeing his mum (and already barely knew his dad). He therefore effectively left home at the age of 8 years old, as he never returned home again to his parents. As a practitioner psychologist I am aware that parental separation in childhood can be traumatic for an individual; however, in the context of the time this was not an unusual situation. My dad certainly doesn't consider this to be traumatic: 'It's just what happened, and that's that!'.

Reflection point 2.1

Having read about the experiences of our families, what thoughts came to you about what you know about your own family?

The impact of sharing stories

The process of thinking about our family members and their experiences across generations led us to consider a number of themes within our clinical work. We noted the importance of appreciating the potential symbolic meaning of presented difficulties and how they are understood by the individual. This led us to further reflect on additional considerations for therapists when working with trauma, and the necessary conditions for facilitating this work. We became aware of the often-overlooked spiritual and transpersonal aspects of an individual's experience, and the potential significance and impact of sharing their personal story.

Understanding symbolic meaning

We considered the importance of understanding the personal meaning of the individual's past, and the potential meaning and function of re-enacted patterns of behaviour from elsewhere. This appreciation may be crucial if there is to be any prospect of clinical change for our clients, no matter how evidence-based our therapeutic approach. If we do not understand the meaning and function of 'the problem', how are we ever to understand why it may be resistant to therapy and change?

Perhaps the unusual (problematic?) behaviour of shaving in the dark may function to reconnect an old soldier with his fallen brothers-in-arms. Why would Grandad Charles not want to feel attached to those other boys who taught him how to survive to be a wise old man (likely an opportunity they were denied)? Traumatic bonding is known to be a particularly powerful form of attachment (Fuselier, 1999), and in certain circumstances is further enhanced if we empathise with our captor or perpetrator (Effiong et al., 2022). In a similar vein, the sense of 'belonging' is a form of attachment considered to be a particularly powerful therapeutic agent in some clinical contexts, such as within the therapeutic community (Pearce & Pickard, 2013).

The act of shaving in the dark may have therefore been accompanied by a deep sense of belonging and camaraderie for Charles, evident in his cheerful explanation of its origins. As we have learned for other veterans with fallen comrades, however, these actions or difficulties making therapeutic gains may also be a gesture of respect, an expression of 'survivor guilt', or of the fear 'lest we forget'.

Some of these patterns of behaviour from the past, or what we term 'rituals', may go unnoticed or indeed be unproblematic, until they come into conflict with the requirements of the present. In this case, Grandad Charles could be left to cheerfully (and perhaps respectfully) shave in the dark within his own home; thankfully, the day never came when he was prevented from doing so by the safety requirements and standards of a care institution.

In considering Nana T's experiences, the description of what she relayed as the 'possession' of family members returning from war, could be understood as a manifestation of psychological distress. This may have taken the form of what we conceptualise as flashbacks and re-enactments. From the Afrocentric context the concepts of 'possession' and 'madness' may be taken to symbolise the way in which those returning from the war ('liberation struggle') appeared set aside from themselves, and from others.

Go curiously: considerations for therapists working with trauma

We wondered whether our grandparents may have been sufficiently affected by the adverse events they experienced for them to be traumatised? We may, of course, not know the true depth to which our beloved family members had been personally affected. Many veterans and survivors of childhood trauma, after all, do their utmost to protect their children from the reality and consequences of what they themselves have endured.

However, we should equally be careful to not presume that experiencing terrible events necessarily equate to a form of PTSD in one's life. The World Health Organisation's International Classification of Diseases (ICD-11, 2022), while formally recognising complex post-traumatic stress disorder (CPTSD) for the first time, is equally clear that the presence or absence of key symptom clusters are the determinants of CPTSD, rather than the nature of the experiences themselves. It would be wise to maintain a respectful curiosity of the differing ways that people may process *potentially* traumatic experiences, and the contribution to this of the groups and culture to which they belong. Some of these means of coping may be beyond our current understanding, and therefore curious attention may extend our personal knowledge, and in turn, our shared knowledge and understanding.

Perhaps born of necessity, and yet building on existing skills, the young boy's careful construction of a model was a helpful coping strategy in the face of loneliness and feelings of abandonment. His coping response and strategy long preceded our clinical appreciation of the effectiveness of mindfulness in the face of emotional distress (Linehan, 1993). His model-making, without intending, also led to friendships with other like-minded (and like-feeling?) boarding schoolboys, and therefore this combination of affect regulation and attachment may explain why he later reported little effect of the separation from his parents.

There may be other examples of how our clients' responses to distress may lead to unexpected outcomes; consider a client with significant dissociation, reported as 'stuck' within the mental health system. It is possible that the relationships they have developed with their care coordinator and practitioner psychologist are (sadly), the most nurturing and containing relationships they have ever known within their life. This may therefore be an important consideration to address constructively with our clients with complex needs if they are to be enabled to outgrow us and graduate from the mental health services. Understandably, much attention is given to stabilisation and safety, and to trauma processing when working with our clients towards recovery from trauma. However, the most overlooked stage of Judith Herman's (1992/2022) phase-based approach to recovering from trauma may indeed be stage three, *Reconnection,* including a reduction of the powerfully isolating effects of traumatic experiences, and the active reengagement with sustaining relationships, activities and personal contributions.

The power of telling the story

It seems we all like a good story and not only when we are children. We may not realise that several western Christmas traditions (e.g., eating turkey) have their origins in the story written by Charles Dickens: *A Christmas Carol* (Dickens, 1868). Dickens himself had a difficult childhood, spending a period within a prison workhouse in London due to his father's debts. As a consequence, he had to leave school and instead work in a shoe polish factory. The adverse childhood experiences of young Dickens could later be seen woven into the lives of characters within his novels, such as Amy Dorritt in *Little Dorritt* (Dickens, 1857). However, despite (or perhaps because of) this, Dicken's ability to tell a good story provided him the equivalent of latter-day 'rock star' fame and wealth. When on tour in the 1860s reading his stories aloud to the audience, he could fill large venues earning himself £80 per night (Forster, 1876).

Sharing our story with others is one of the earliest recognised means of processing a traumatic experience, and has been practised for centuries within the traditions of oral history in Eastern and African cultures (Abrams, 2016). These traditions, whether of Eastern or Western origin, have not remained unchanged, however. The passing of time and the increased mobility of subsequent generations has impinged on these cultural traditions, sometimes with serious and unexpected consequences. It has been suggested that many indigenous Australian people have developed a significant problem of transgenerational trauma following their colonisation, but importantly, this has been exacerbated by a moving away from the potentially mediating effects of their shared indigenous cultural identities, values and traditions (The Healing Foundation, 2011); see Key resources and further reading.

Peter Fonagy and his colleagues have explored the potential interrelationship between learning from the stories and knowledge of others, attachment and mental health (Fonagy et al., 2019). They suggest that a specific form of trust they refer to as *epistemic trust* is the mediating factor that determines whether we permit ourselves to quickly learn important social information from the experience and knowledge offered to us by others, or we have a *mistrust* of this. Fonagy et al. (2019) suggest our ability to experience epistemic trust is influenced by our developmental experiences of the reliability and the benign intentions of others, i.e. our attachment experiences. In other words, if we were fortunate to have experienced good, reliable, consistent responses from others early in our lives then we are more likely to trust the social learning that others offer later in our lives. You may already be considering the implications this may have for the inter-personal learning we offer our clients within therapeutic work and for our understanding of our clients' difficulties in changing quickly.

Peter Fonagy himself was not always a celebrated practitioner psychologist and psychoanalyst; he too has a story he has shared (BBC Radio 4, 2020); see Key resources and further reading, from which we all might learn. He arrived alone in the UK following political unrest in Hungary, at the age of 15 years. He did not speak any English, and understandably found his relocation, bullying at school and social isolation a significant challenge. He developed suicidal thoughts but fortunately was able to be referred to a therapist, who was a psy-choanalyst. He derived great benefit from this therapy and the therapeutic relationship, within which he felt his therapist 'met' his mind.

He later studied psychology, trained as a clinical psychologist and later as a psychoanalyst. Together with colleagues, he went on to develop a new thera-peutic approach building on attachment theory: mentalisation-based therapy (Bateman & Fonagy, 2004; Bateman et al., 2019; Bateman et al., 2023). Peter Fonagy's professional contribution is as impressive as his personal story is inspiring.

Sharing our story may not only be potentially helpful to others, but also lead us to appreciate 'new' aspects of the context to the events we are relating to. As I (MM) talked with fellow authors about my grandparents and re-read my writ-ten account of this, it was the first time that I considered the racial discrimination experienced within my own (White Irish) family history. As I write now, I won-der about the possible inter-generational manifestations of this; my mother's frequently expressed concern about what our neighbours might think; and then what of my own desire to impress others?

The clinical implications of this are intriguing, and a source of hope for practi-tioner psychologists. Most of the therapeutic approaches we employ entail a sharing of the traumatic story within a trusted relationship and a containing space. Dual Representation Theory (Brewin and Burgess, 1996, 2014) suggests that the develop-ment of a verbally-based, contextualised representation of the traumatising experience can become the neurologically preferred memory, rather than the intru-sive sensory-based fragments of the earlier traumatic memory. In other words, being able to form a story of the event that can be articulated, and which includes a place and time context, can come to 'trump' the dislocated sensory fragments of reexperiencing when it comes to our future remembering.

Visual imagery is also known to be a potentially powerful medium of change (Kroener et al., 2023), even if the imagery is known by us to not accurately reflect the actual events we have experienced. Therapeutic work addressing intrusive imagery may be effective in reducing the risk of developing PTSD (Deforges et al., 2023), or with reducing the symptom severity of established PTSD (Asselbergs et al., 2023).

Many years ago, I (MM) worked with a man whose son had drowned in a shipping accident some five years earlier. He had not been present to directly witness this but appeared as if vicariously traumatised; tortured by recurring intrusive images of his son trapped and slowly drowning. This traumatic imag-ery (as commonly is the case) had prevented him from being able to grieve the loss of his son. His intrusive traumatic imagery could be easily triggered by everyday activities, such as the sound of water from him turning on a tap. In the absence of grieving, he also suffered a repeated, unprocessed sense of shock of having lost his son. These combined effects were leading to his own metaphorical drowning, as he became increasingly debilitated and unable to function within his life.

At that time, I was primarily working within an exposure-based approach with his 'traumatic memory', while feeling a little uncomfortable that this memory was not of the more familiar directly experienced kind (as he had not been present). During one, seemingly unhelpful, session, I found myself reflecting more deeply about the possible actual experience of drowning, assisted by the reports of others who had been revived in the past after the loss of consciousness. Drowning I wondered, perhaps was not necessarily an endless tortured process, but one which may move on to a sense of peace in our final moments. I clearly don't know this to have been the case for his son, but I shared this thought and the possibility with my client. His creativity and resilience readily grasped at this, and he 'swam with it'. He described his own imagery of what this peaceful death may have been like for his son, and I suggested he replay this imagery in his mind between sessions. The next time we met he smiled warmly at me from behind his tears, and told me he was now grieving.

It is important for us to continue to seek new possibilities for therapeutic work; one of these areas of research (Deforges et al., 2023) seeks to develop interventions that specifically target crucial psychological components of traumatic memory. Whilst these potentially highly accessible, brief, mechanism-focused interventions are exciting developments in the clinical field, it remains to be seen whether they can be sufficient to address the multi-faceted nature of complex PTSD of many of our clients. We discuss the current research and derived understanding of the nature of complex trauma further in Chapter 5.

Facilitating conditions for therapeutic trauma work

There are many subtle, yet challenging, relational processes that may be potentially impactful when helping people to work through their traumatic experiences. These relational processes may include:

- feeling sufficiently safe and contained with another person that we might risk openly facing the worst moments of our life
- permitting the unspeakable we have known to be spoken, heard and witnessed
- giving voice to our silently wounding shame and self-blame.

However, one of the aspects of the therapeutic relationship with which we are most familiar is the tangible empathy of the therapist. Tangible, because we imagine our client needs to be aware of our willingness and capacity to understand and enter their world and experience.

One of the lessons I learned (MM) from several decades of working with clients and their trauma is, if you are to really understand, you and your client have to be there, rather than look on from afar. By this I mean being able and willing to enter, back where and when 'it' happened, appreciating both the figure and the ground of the traumatic events. Traumatised people often infer self-critical meaning or unwarranted self-blame due to the information-processing difficulties associated with being overwhelmed. The nature of overwhelming experience is that it is accompanied by a narrowing of our attentional focus and conceptual understanding. Brewin and colleagues suggest this is related to the way our brain functions under these high arousal conditions (Brewin et al., 2014). While this perceptual narrowing has no doubt evolved to support our physical survival, it does little to support our psychological wellbeing afterwards (perhaps that evolved response is still in progress?). We can often be left with a severely limited reflective understanding of what actually happened, why it happened, and any contributing systemic and contextual factors.

Therefore, a second lesson enters the frame; to be therapeutically helpful, we have to be there with our client, and also, *not* be fully there. Consider the metaphor; in the moment when your client is hanging off the mountain facing and fearing death, they can also sense the warm, firm grip of your hand, trust your benevolent intent and hear your encouraging and hopeful perspective from your solid ground. If our client feels we too may fall off the mountain if they share their story, they may well seek to protect us from a similar fate. This containing stance may understandably be difficult to develop as a therapist or practitioner psychologist for a variety of reasons. We may have similar personal experiences rekindled by their story that we still need to address ourselves; we may be relatively new to the powerful emotions and relational dynamics of trauma work; or we may simply not have had many experiences (yet) of the inspiring, transformative change that is possible. If reading this is proving of benefit to you, then you have the many clients to thank who taught us to feel hopeful and be quietly confident about the change that is possible by going there with your client, while also remaining here in the present.

But what could help us develop and maintain this 'firm footing' that, in turn, may facilitate our therapeutic effectiveness in working with traumatised people? There are likely to be a number of factors, but there is evidence that this may include the relationships we have within our working environment. It was noted many years ago that the rates of 'shell-shock' among different battalions similarly facing the frontline varied considerably, and this appeared to vary depending on the group cohesiveness of the battalion. This was more recently confirmed in a large sample of troops deployed to conflict zones in Iraq and Afghanistan (Keller, 2005). Pre-deployment trauma, and frequent exposure to trauma once deployed, were found to be good predictors of soldiers' perceived stress. However, group cohesion and social support moderated the effect of this stress and the positive psychological adaptation to the potentially stressful environments.

What of the implications of this in contemporary mental health settings and teams? Trauma-informed care teams have been described as services which examine the systems, policies and processes that support (rather than mitigate against) therapeutic trauma work. This should include attention to the support, supervision and mentorship of the practitioner psychologist and their team colleagues. A meta-analysis of studies of trauma-informed care systems supported the potentially beneficial effects of these for their service personnel and for the effectiveness of their therapeutic work (Fernández et al., 2023). There is a well-worn management cliché that says, *'There is no I in Team!'*. Given that practitioner psychologists are social beings, working with relational trauma in a relational way within a service context, perhaps there really is no 'I' in the trauma-informed team?

Spiritual and transpersonal aspects

We clearly need to take care to reflect on the potential contribution of differences, or similarities, of our clients' spiritual beliefs to our own (Currier et al., 2023). It is evident that our clients can be affected at an emotional, physical and social level as a result of their overwhelming experiences, and also simultaneously deeply affected at a spiritual level.

Currier (2022) considered the effect of our own violations of our personal code and sense of morality in what has been termed *moral injury.* It is also known that moral injury can also be associated with a sense of betrayal (considered further in Chapter 8). We can feel protected and nurtured by the system to which we feel we belong, and we can also feel abandoned and betrayed within this relationship. We may therefore be reminded of the complex, yet subtle, detrimental consequences potentially inflicted by trauma. This may become apparent within our therapeutic work with clients.

When one of us (DC) was working with an asylum seeker who had been tortured, the man recounted the horrific torture he had been subjected to and added *'When they did that to me ... that's when my soul fell out'.*

Another colleague (EB) recalls working with a man who had a heart attack and a serious head injury that resulted in a severe traumatic brain injury. As he walked around the unit it appeared to her that it was almost as if he was just a physical body; *that his soul had dropped out of him.* If we are indeed bio-psycho-social-spiritual beings, then it may be wise to pay attention to all aspects of our being, and how traumatic experiences may manifest (O'Brien & Charura, 2023).

In our clinical experience we have known many clients who have, perhaps hesitantly, shared an account of their out-of-body experience. Their hesitancy may have alluded to a fear of either judgement, shaming, proclamation of madness, or to an unspoken norm of our contemporary relating. As practitioner psychologists we need to strive to create and maintain the conditions necessary to feel able to speak of these experiences.

But how are we to understand these disembodied accounts of being able to 'look on' at the scene, as if from an anaesthetised, distant perspective? It is known that shifts in our physical homeostasis (through starvation, dehydration, sleep deprivation, extreme temperature, etc.) can result in dissociative-like symptoms of depersonalisation/derealisation (American Psychiatric Association, 2022). In addition, certain substances have long been favoured, and sometimes feared, for their potential mind-altering properties. However, a marked threat or shift in our psychological homeostasis may of itself be sufficient to produce dissociative symptoms, including out-of-body experiences. These threats or states may include overwhelming helplessness, extreme anxiety or fear, or perceived or actual existential threat.

However, this is the view offered through a Western-scientific-mechanistic lens; additional lenses are available and readily engaged by other cultures and communities. Thus peri-traumatic experience (i.e. during the event) can be the catalyst for out-of-body experience, whether it be understood as due to physical, emotional/psychological, or spiritual causation.

As practitioner psychologists who have worked with traumatised people for many years, we acknowledge that some of this clinical understanding may be coming from 'a different place': a frame of reference steeped in an openness to the complexity of the human condition, and how we might respond to it with acknowledgement of the transpersonal, collective unconscious or embodied dimensions.

The stories of our grandparents were fascinating and inspiring for us to share with each other, but at another deeper level maybe we already knew and had assimilated these? Indeed, perhaps these are the reasons we choose to work with traumatised people and find ourselves together writing about trauma?

Reflective Questions:

- How often do you enquire about your clients' grandparents and their lives within your assessment?
- How may this offer additional understanding of the client who is currently on your mind?
- How might you plan for the third stage (of phase-based model) *Reconnection* to become more integrated within your therapeutic work with traumatised people?

3 What is trauma?

Emma Bradshaw, Divine Charura and Mark McFetridge

Overview

- This chapter will explore the different aspects of what trauma is.
- It will consider biological, psychological, social, sexual, spiritual and cultural aspects of trauma and assert that trauma can be a complex interplay of these factors.
- We emphasise the importance of considering the wider context when working relationally with those who have experienced trauma.

In Chapter 2 we outlined the historical context of how our understanding of psychological trauma came about and we shared some examples and reflections from our own experiences as an illustration of this. In this chapter we will look further into some of the many different aspects of trauma. We will first consider the definition of trauma, before introducing some of the theories and classifications of trauma. We will then think carefully about how trauma can be explained from a variety of different perspectives, which include biological, psychological, social and cultural factors. We move on to acknowledge how trauma can be a complex interplay of many of these factors and emphasise the importance of considering the wider context when working relationally with clients who are trying to cope with their individual experience of trauma.

Definition and classification of trauma

The word 'trauma' is derived from the Latin *traumaticus* and the Greek *traumatikos*, meaning 'wound'. While this originally referred to physical wounds, the meaning has been extended to encompass psychological injury too.

A (potentially) traumatic event always happens within a context, and it is the interaction and interplay of these contextual factors that determine the nature of our wound. These factors might be divided into those relating to:

- our personhood (e.g., our attachment history, our values and meaning making, our previous experience of trauma, our personal and relational resources)
- the event itself (e.g., the unexpectedness and horror entailed, whether interpersonal, and our relationship to the perpetrator)
- what follows the event (e.g. the responses of others, traumatic bereavement, physical injury in addition to our psychological wounding)

There are several classifications and taxonomies of trauma which have been proposed by different experts in the field. As these classifications are commonly referred to, it is useful to have a brief overview of what they are to aid understanding and assessment of trauma.

One well-known classification system was proposed by Lenore Terr (Terr, 1988), a psychiatrist and trauma expert who worked with children. Terr proposed the popular concept of 'Type I' and 'Type II' trauma. Type I trauma, also referred to as single incident trauma, occurs in a time-limited framework: examples include accidents, natural disasters or a one-off act of violence. Type II trauma is also referred to as complex, or prolonged, trauma and involves prolonged exposure to traumatic events which often occurred within a relational or interpersonal context and then stopped. Examples include ongoing abuse, neglect or exposure to domestic violence. A third type of trauma, Type III, has been proposed by Ibrahim Kira (Kira, 2001) and refers to traumas which happen over a prolonged period, possibly even a lifetime.

Another taxonomy of trauma, outlined by Kira (2022) focuses on individual functioning and includes attachment trauma, identity trauma, interdependence/disconnectedness trauma, self-actualisation trauma and survival trauma. We would add to this by including relational trauma, racial trauma and vicarious trauma. Below, we briefly summarise each:

1 **Attachment trauma** is early childhood trauma that occurs through an absence of connectedness from caregiver to child, resulting in a lack of security and trust in the child. This experience can affect the way that a child forms relationships and can impact beliefs about self and emotional processing.
2 **Identity trauma** can occur as a child moves from adolescence to adulthood, a time when they would ideally be able to develop a sense of identity and autonomy. If this is disrupted it can result in a sense of loss of self and helplessness.
3 **Interdependence/disconnectedness trauma** can happen if an individual experiences a sense of social connectedness which is then suddenly removed

(e.g. by moving schools or becoming a refugee); it is an experience that can be deeply unsettling or traumatising for the individual.

4 **Self-actualisation trauma** may present in those whose sense of self-worth is linked to what they achieve. When this is not possible (e.g. loss of job, money, health, etc.) it can be perceived as traumatic.

5 **Survival trauma** can happen following a time when an individual experiences or witnesses a traumatic event that is threatening to themselves or significant others.

6 **Relational trauma** includes 'the experience of the severing, fragmenting and/or violating of a significant relationship (s)' (Smith & Charura, 2024, pp. 100–101).

7 **Racial trauma** refers to 'psychological, physiological, and behavioural responses to race-based threats and discriminatory experiences' (Holmes et al., 2024). We will expand on this understanding in Chapter 5.

8 **Vicarious trauma** may occur during the process of hearing about trauma from others. This new information may affect the individual by challenging their knowledge of the world and challenging their view of themselves, others and the world around them (McNeillie and Rose, 2021). It is important for therapists to be aware of this type of trauma so that support can be sought when necessary.

In Chapter 6 we will outline the different diagnostic categories of trauma in greater detail. However, it is worth mentioning here that when we are considering what trauma is, it is important to remember that trauma is *not* simply a list of symptoms; it will present differently in every individual due to several reasons. Traumatic events can be experienced differently from one person to another…what is traumatic for one person may not be traumatic for another. For example, if two people were inside a building which was on fire, both might find the experience frightening, but one might recover afterwards whereas the other might go on to develop PTSD. This could be for reasons including the personality of the individual (as some personality types have been found to recover from trauma more easily than others; see Jayawickreme et al., 2021) and whether they have experienced previous trauma.

Having summarised some of the types of trauma above, it is important to note that some are more likely than others to co-occur. In a study which explored the links between trauma experiences and dissociation and psychopathology, Schimmenti (2018) found that attachment trauma often co-occurs with other experiences of trauma later in life. Also, those who have multiple traumatic experiences are at a greater risk of psychopathology. The experience of dissociation can be a way of coping for those who have had early traumatic experiences. It is thought that dissociation may be a protective mechanism which can temporarily help those experiencing trauma to distance themselves from the unbearable reality of the thoughts, feelings, memories and behaviours that they are experiencing. However, when dissociation is activated in a sustained or repeated way it can become pathological and link to psychopathology.

A biological perspective

Despite trauma being a psychological 'wound', the first outward sign indicating that a person is traumatised may be physical. The somatisation may therefore manifest what we understand as biological symptoms of trauma. This was first acknowledged by German neurologist Hermann Oppenheim (1858–1919), who introduced the concept of 'traumatic neurosis' in 1889 after observing psychological trauma experienced from accidents on the railways, and later the 'shell shock' or 'neurasthenia' suffered by the soldiers returning from the First World War, in 1914 to 1918. Those who were not executed for supposed cowardice, and sacrificed as a warning to others, experienced symptoms that are little-known today. There were frequent cases of paralysis of the lower limbs, or of unusual gait, shaking bodies as well as hysterical blindness. In 1917, Oppenheim acknowledged that psychological shock could lead to a physical reaction, due to activation of the 'vasomotor-secretory-trophic nervous system' which we now refer to as the autonomic nervous system (Linden & Jones, 2013).

Neuroscience research has continued to develop since this time, and we have a greater understanding of the autonomic nervous system and the somatisation of trauma. We now know that our nervous system is made up of billions of neurons (nerve cells) which send messages throughout our body to regulate involuntary physiological functions such as heart rate, blood pressure, respiratory rate and digestion. The autonomic nervous system has two branches: sympathetic and parasympathetic. The sympathetic nervous system is often associated with the 'fight or flight' response, preparing the body to deal with stressors or threats, whereas the parasympathetic nervous system is often associated with the 'rest and digest' response, promoting relaxation and recovery (Weissman & Mendes, 2021).

A related theory which aids our understanding of how trauma affects our bodies is polyvagal theory, developed by neuroscientist and psychophysiologist Dr Stephen Porges in 1997 (Porges, 2017). Polyvagal theory is a complex concept that explains how our nervous system influences our emotional and physiological responses, especially in social situations. It suggests that our bodies 'reactions are controlled by a complex network of nerves, particularly the vagus nerve, which can trigger different states including fight-or-flight, shutdown or engagement with others.

Polyvagal theory acknowledges the importance of connection with others, and a key component to facilitate this is the social engagement system (Porges, 2017) which is associated with the parasympathetic nervous system. When we are engaged with another person, sharing eye contact, a smile and soft voice tones, the vagus nerve mediates via the muscles of the eyes, ears, face and larynx to enable us to feel safe and calm (Taylor, 2014). However, if we are living in an environment which feels unsafe, the body will experience a sense of threat and may immobilise. Porges (2017) refers to this neural process of evaluating risk in the environment without awareness as 'neuroception'.

Polyvagal theory has a valuable role to play in understanding and treating mental health conditions. By adding a polyvagal perspective to clinical practice, clinicians are more able to support their traumatised clients to feel safe and supported, to become more regulated and to begin to build pathways to engage in positive social interactions and facilitate communication and safety in relationships (Dana, 2018, 2021). This has led to interventions to address the somatic experiencing of trauma, with recommendations to therapists of the importance of integrating body-oriented approaches (such as yoga) with traditional talking therapy (Rothschild, 2000; van der Kolk, 2014).

Another biological aspect of trauma is the way in which trauma can be passed down from one generation to the next and is the subject of a growing body of research (Yehuda & Lehrner, 2018). An important biological aspect of this is the role of epigenetics: the study of how behaviour and environment can change the way that genes function. Related concepts are those of intergenerational and transgenerational trauma, which is the subconscious transmission of trauma symptoms from one generation to another. In a paper which reviewed the research evidence concerning the intergenerational transmission of trauma effects and the possible role of epigenetic mechanisms in this transmission, Yehuda and Lehrner (2018) identified two broad categories of epigenetic effects: developmentally programmed effects and preconception trauma effects. The former occur because of the offsprings early environmental exposures (e.g. the mother's stress during and after pregnancy), whereas the latter is concerned with epigenetic changes in parents due to trauma before conception. These concepts can be controversial and will be discussed in Chapter 11, where we consider epigenetics and the transgenerational transmission of trauma in greater depth.

Other studies that have explored the biological impact of trauma have been conducted with children who lived in Romanian orphanages and spent their early days lying in their cots without being picked up and cuddled. These children experienced the trauma of emotional neglect which stunted their growth both biologically and neurologically (Johnson et al., 1992). However, the children who were adopted into families went on to develop almost as well as the children of the family, as they settled into their life with their new families, suggesting that the biological impacts are not irreversible (Morison & Ellwood, 2000). This relates to the relatively new concept of neuroplasticity where, with repeated use, the nervous system has the ability to change its activity and reorganise its structure, functions or connections: 'neurons that fire together, wire together' (van der Kolk, 2014).

Knowledge of the biological impact of trauma leads us to reflect at a wider level, referring to the biological concept of assimilation, whereby a living organism incorporates external substances into their cells or tissues. For example, we can consider old trees. We can have a great respect for ancient trees because they have been through difficult times, just as humans have been through difficult times. They have been affected by climate change, and by the comings and goings around them, even wars, and yet they continue to grow and are shaped at some points. What they have been through in recent years is more evident, whereas what they went through 50 or 100 years ago is less evident – the link between their experiences and their shape is less obvious. It can be a parallel process for humans: we can be shaped by past experiences which are less obvious but impact us in the present and we can consider what we are carrying from previous generations within ourselves. Early experiences may help us to conceptualise what happens to us when we experience trauma and how we emotionally regulate both through it and afterwards. And, like trees, sometimes it would benefit us to turn to face the light in a different way!

A psychological perspective

The experience of trauma can have a profound psychological impact too. It has been found that people who reported to have experienced trauma due to physical, sexual or emotional abuse in childhood, went on to experience trauma in other forms later in life (van der Kolk, 1989). Something that we have observed in our clinical work with traumatised clients is their tendency to repeat the trauma they have experienced by unconsciously putting themselves in similar situations; for example, someone who experienced childhood abuse might find themselves in an abusive adult relationship. In an article which explored this tendency to repeat, Bessel van der Kolk (1989) explained how trauma is repeated on behavioural, emotional, physiologic and neuroendocrinologic levels. The behaviours associated with this repetition include how those who were harmed then go on to harm themselves. Alternatively, they may engage in self-destructiveness with behaviours such as biting, burning, headbanging and cutting. Van der Kolk (1989) also suggests that revictimisation may occur where abused boys are more likely to identify with the aggressor and become abusive towards others, whereas abused girls tend to have relationships with abusive men and continue to be abused. They are also more likely to engage in drug abuse, prostitution and suicide attempts. While this refers to heterosexual relationships, the suggestion is that at an emotional level, after the experience of abuse, life is never the same again. Those who have been abused as a child often direct anger towards themselves, as it is too dangerous to direct it outwards, towards their abuser who may also be their caregiver. Anger may continue to present in adulthood, without awareness that this is a re-enactment of the past.

Another psychological aspect that can present is traumatic bonding. When faced with danger, it is a natural human response to seek comfort in relationships. If a loving relationship is not available, the victim may turn to their abuser instead. This can happen in adults as well as children, often to the confusion of others. When an act of violence is followed by reconciliation and forgiveness, this reinforces the relationship bond, and so the pattern continues. This psychological response is often seen in settings of domestic abuse: if a child grows up in an abusive environment, they learn to expect the pattern of periods of calm alternating with violent outbursts and a sustained period of calm is unfamiliar (van der Kolk, 1989).

Social and cultural perspectives

Having considered biological and psychological perspectives, it is also important to acknowledge the experience of trauma from a wider, societal viewpoint. Here, we will consider the cultural variations in the way that trauma is experienced and the implications this may have on trauma treatment.

The power of the culturally held beliefs which underpin health may be illustrated by the example of HIV and AIDS in diverse communities. In this example, we describe how being diagnosed with this condition in itself can be traumatic and have a devastating effect. There was a general belief for many years that if somebody received a diagnosis of HIV, then their life was over. We are aware of family friends and distant relatives who were given a diagnosis of HIV and then died within a relatively short space of time. It was as if the community belief and collective unconscious was that once you have this dreaded disease of AIDS, you are dead. The lay language we have often heard used in different context when supporting families and partners/spouses includes phrases such as the person 'gave up', or 'lost hope', they 'gave up the fight' or 'gave up on life'. However, the mind–body paradigm and neuroscience may shed some light here. The cingulate gyrus in the limbic system (associated with emotion) also influences respiration and breathing, and so it is possible that ultimately the individual may have a cardiac arrest from the shock of finding out that they have this (formerly incurable) disease (Bailey, 2021).

In current times, however, the way we think about HIV has changed now that new treatments such as antiretroviral therapy (ART) are available. In our work with patients who have a diagnosis of HIV or who are going through HIV treatment we can observe different cultural discourses: it is now known that it is possible to live for years with HIV so sudden death is less likely. The response to trauma in the case described above could potentially be framed as medically unexplained symptoms where persistent bodily complaints cannot easily be accounted for upon medical examination. Other examples are the cases of paralysis in war veterans, mentioned above, which may be difficult to account for medically and may give us another vantage point on the experience of trauma.

Another example of cultural variation in the experience of trauma symptoms relates to the menopause. The period from perimenopause (i.e. when the body starts to lose hormones and transition to menopause) to menopause itself (i.e. the time of life when periods stop due to low hormones) can last for several years. The average age range for experiencing perimenopause is 45 to 55 years, but it can be earlier. For some women, this time of their lives can be distressing, and even traumatic, as biological changes often coincide with life events such as caring for teenage children and elderly parents. There is emerging evidence to suggest that adverse childhood experiences (ACEs) can contribute to heightened distress in perimenopause (Kapoor et al., 2021). This information is important because the rates of suicide in perimenopausal women are higher than other age groups of women. In a study that investigated suicidal ideation across the reproductive life cycle of women in six European countries, Usall et al. (2009) found an increased risk of suicidal ideation in perimenopausal women. A study of Korean women of perimenopausal and menopausal age also indicated increased depressive symptoms and suicidality in this population (An et al., 2022). However, there can be cultural variations in the experience of menopause. Chinese women have been found to place a different emphasis on the difficulties of menopause: rather than a mainly biological focus, they viewed this transition as part of the experience of midlife (Adler et al., 2000). It is possible that this is but one example of a difference in the cultural understanding of the manifestation of the menopause leading to a differing awareness, attributions of meaning and consequent reporting of this (Melby et al., 2005). There may, however, be other factors such as dietary differences that also contribute (e.g. the consumption of soya) to these cultural differences. Overall, the links between menopause symptoms and trauma are still to be understood, with both variations and similarities in symptomology across cultures (Obermeyer, 2000). It is certainly important to ask women of this age group about their experience of menopause when they present in therapy to ensure that this factor is not overlooked in the context of their trauma history.

Consideration of culture is not only important in the understanding the impact of trauma, but also in the assessment and treatment of trauma symptoms too. Cultural variations in the experience of trauma have been acknowledged when diagnosing PTSD and CPTSD. In Chapter 6 we will talk more about the diagnosis of trauma and we note that, while diagnosis may not always be necessary or applicable when trying to help a client who presents in therapy wanting help to manage their trauma-related difficulties, it can be helpful to have this classification in mind as a framework within which to explore the role of culture in their lives. In a paper which adopted a cross-cultural approach to assessing trauma reactions, Patel and Hall (2021) acknowledged that trauma reactions can vary considerably across cultures. They recommended the following:

1 A need for culturally sensitive instruments as additions to the traditional trauma assessment approaches
2 A stance of cultural humility when administering assessments
3 Knowledge of how to account for ongoing trauma and adversity
4 Incorporating the findings into treatment

Overall, it is important to acknowledge that a culturally sensitive approach is needed when working clinically with those who experience trauma, rather than assuming that Western assessments and diagnoses should be applied everywhere. Maintaining a respectful, curious stance can help to improve the quality of care for those with mental health difficulties worldwide.

Spiritual perspectives

In this chapter, we have started to consider how trauma impacts us biologically, psychologically, socially and culturally, however one aspect which is often missed is the spiritual impact of trauma. We have heard clients from diverse ethnic communities talk about trauma as a 'soul wound'. They have used the quote from the Bible: 'And fear ye not them that kill the body and are not able to kill the soul: but rather fear him that can destroy both soul and body in hell' [Matthew 10:28].

We have come across survivors of torture who have spoken about how the perpetrators were doing harm to their body, but they were able to survive because they knew they couldn't touch their soul. While you could interpret this as denial, or a defence, it is important to honour the spiritual belief that it is only when their soul has been touched that the trauma prevails.

The experience of dreaming can also have a spiritual perspective in relation to processing trauma. In his papers on the interpretation of dreams (Freud, 1900), Freud suggests that dreams are how the psyche processes that which is unconscious, or that which has just permeated consciousness. This understanding also links to what is thought to happen in rapid eye movement (REM) or dream sleep, where it is suggested that dreams are a way of processing the events that we experience in life to move them comfortably into the past, a concept that is used to inform eye movement desensitisation and reprocessing (EMDR) therapy (Shapiro, 2017)

However, while this can be a helpful way of understanding the role of dreams, Nwoye (2017) suggests that this focus on the individual is a Eurocentric way of interpreting dreams. African psychology suggests an alternative approach: that dreams are an indication of what is to come. We are aware of people who have dreamt when seriously ill in hospital, and the subject that was dreamt about did happen. In addition to this, dreams can have a collective nature, where people who are connected dream with the same epistemology. Spiritually, therefore, dreams can help someone to be prepared for a traumatic experience, which can lead to more effective processing of the trauma afterwards. Asking clients about their dreams in trauma therapy and holding an open mind in relation to the meaning they attach to their experience is therefore important and can help therapists to work more effectively with those from different cultural backgrounds.

Final reflections

This chapter leads us to wonder how we perceive trauma and how the current understanding of trauma may be missing the point. We may demonstrate awareness of biological, psychological, social, cultural and spiritual aspects of trauma, but actually the experience of the traumatised individual, or traumatised group, will incorporate a complex interplay of many of these factors. It is understood that the French neurologist, Jean-Martin Charcot (1825–1893) said that hysteria was elusive: changing in form as soon as it is approached (Kundu, 2004). Likewise, thinking about what trauma is and try to categorise it, or make it fit into a diagnostic box, changes its form because we focus too much on the content (i.e. about what happened, and the symptoms experienced). In doing this, we are in danger of missing the phenomenological experience of the individual who is experiencing the effects of trauma.

We therefore encourage a curiosity about the lived experience of trauma for the individual which incorporates their cultural experience including multiple truths. We can see that even diagnostic manuals (see Chapter 6 for further information) differ in their definition of trauma, and these definitions are likely to change in the future as research in the area develops. Trauma is therefore not necessarily a condition to be 'boxed' and diagnosed but it is a more fluid process, encompassing multiple aspects.

So, we can appreciate the complexity of the situation. Those trying to apply the diagnostic criteria for trauma must accommodate multiple factors: they can identify symptoms which may meet the current criteria, but of primary importance is the need to validate the experience of the individual. Sometimes the symptoms of the individual may not meet the current diagnostic criteria for PTSD, however it does not mean that their experience is any less distressing. We could therefore conceptualise the lexicon of the diagnostic criteria as one of many pathways to helping us to understand the person's truth, rather than the diagnosis of PTSD being the endpoint that the person must live with forever.

A common question often asked by clients attending therapy to help them to manage their trauma symptoms is: 'Will I ever recover from trauma?'. Many therapeutic models suggest that individuals can be treated 'for trauma', but it may be prudent to ask ourselves whether "recover" is the best word to use here. In Chapter 12 we talk in greater detail about the concept of post-traumatic growth, where individuals may learn to live in a way that is different from the way they lived before the traumatic experience. Living in a new way for the rest of their lives may be challenging for some, as they may be living with a physical or psychological injury which means that life will never be the same again. For others, new ways of coping, linked to their values, may be established and they may live their life differently, for example by working less, or by developing different ways of relating: they may therefore live better than before and present as 'treated' or 'recovered', however while a shift or change can happen, this may be different from recovery.

So, the message that we would like to convey to our readers is to remain curious and to have an open mind about what trauma is. It is important to think about the individual person, in their unique circumstances: rather than trying to narrow down the concept of trauma, consider how the person in front of you is describing their experiences. While the person in front of you might meet the diagnostic criteria for PTSD, it is important to consider them as a whole person, in the context of their environment. By adopting a curious mind, you could contribute to the future understanding of trauma by noticing something which otherwise might be discarded because it doesn't neatly fit into the trauma 'box'. To illustrate these points, in Chapter 4 we will introduce three case studies to illustrate the points we have made above. We will follow these cases as we go into greater depth about these trauma-related concepts throughout the book.

Reflection point 3.1

1 What new information about trauma have you learnt from reading this chapter?
2 How might an understanding of trauma be integrated into your clinical practice?
3 What aspects of trauma knowledge would you like to learn more about?

4 | Cases from 50 years of practice

Divine Charura, Mark McFetridge, Emma Bradshaw

Overview

- This chapter will present three cases of people whose lives and experiences will be woven throughout the book, to help interlink the concepts we discuss.
- It will cover considerations on trauma, vicarious trauma and the mind–body connection and trauma across the lifespan.
- We emphasise the importance of considering the family and social context when working relationally with those who have experienced trauma.

Introduction

In this chapter we will introduce the people (cases) whose lives and experiences will be woven throughout the book, to help interlink the concepts we discuss. As noted in Chapter 1, we have formulated the fictitious cases we present in this chapter in a way that maintains the authentic nature of different traumas that many people presenting in different contexts we have worked with may experience. Furthermore, we weave in the importance of valuing social constructs such as gender, sexuality, social class and economic factors, age, dis/ability and ethnicity (Moodley, 2009; Winter & Charura, 2023). We also highlight the importance of intersectionality as it relays our perspective that a person is not just a 'white man' or 'white woman' or a 'Black man' and so on, but that they may simultaneously identify across different social constructs and identities. For example, an individual can be a Black man, identifying as heterosexual, of Christian/Islamic faith, identifying with a particular social class etc. Crenshaw (1991) argued that intersectionality recognises that socially constructed identity categories (e.g. race, class, gender and sexual orientation) simultaneously interact with each other and with wider societal and power structures to construct experiences of oppression and privilege unique to each individual.

In line with this, Winter and Charura (2023) in their writing on social justice argued that engaging with intersectionality illuminates the complexities and tensions or dynamics of oppression/being othered/dislocation and connection/ belonging and privilege. Thus, in us linking these perspectives with our approach to working with trauma and the cases that are to be presented in this chapter we highlight the importance of holding in mind the environment within which individuals and communities dwell. We agree with the critique that Feltham and Horton (2000) offered that the psychological professions can be rightly criticised for focusing on the psychology of the individual and their internal life while ignoring the impact of the social, economic and cultural environment in which people live (Feltham & Horton, 2000: 24).

From the summation of our years of practice which tallies to over 50 years, and in considering the review of research literature as presented in Chapter 5, we agree that in many cases if an individual has experienced trauma earlier on in life this has implications. For example, if they have not had the support for it to be resolved or worked through, and if they then face other significant traumas, they are highly likely to experience post-traumatic stress symptoms or complex post-traumatic stress.

In Chapter 3 we reflected on the mind–body connection impact of trauma. In this chapter we make reference to the point that those who have experienced childhood trauma are more likely to have certain physical/health conditions and psychological trauma can impact us physically through life (van der Kolk, 2014). An example we have often discussed is how an abused child or a young girl who has experienced sexual abuse, for instance, will enter puberty earlier, and this will then cascade in terms of how she engages socially or fits in or not in her social group. This early development into puberty resulting from the trauma she experienced may then mean that she is vulnerable to unwanted sexual advances, which may lead to further trauma. In line with this, data from the UK Office for National Statistics (2017) reported that individuals who were abused as children are more likely to be abused as an adult. According to the Crime Survey for England and Wales (CSEW) for the year ending March 2016, around one in five adults aged 16 to 59 years (an estimated 6.2 million people) had experienced some form of abuse as a child, The reported data also highlighted that a higher proportion of survivors of child abuse went on to experience domestic abuse in adulthood, compared with those who suffered no childhood abuse. Survivors of psychological and physical abuse, sexual assault and witnessing domestic abuse were the most likely to suffer domestic abuse; 77 per cent of the sample had experienced domestic abuse after the age of 16, compared with 40 per cent who experienced one type of abuse as a child. Almost a third (31 per cent) of adults who were abused as a child reported also being sexually assaulted as an adult, compared with 7 per cent of those who did not experience abuse as a child (ONS, 2017).

Trauma and vicarious trauma: the mind–body connection

We have through our clinical practice, supported women who have shared how trauma has impacted their menstrual cycle and potentially triggered early menopause. With this awareness we have about trauma, in our clinical practice we have where appropriate explored with clients/patients their experience of menstruation following trauma. Such exploration can include, for example, asking when an individual had their first menstrual cycle. In discussing examples of the presentation of this in clinical practice we all had narratives of women sharing with us in trauma therapy that they experienced their few first menstrual cycles without any guidance or support from anyone/primary care givers and that they had to deal with it on their own for up to two years. These clients/patients were sharing these narratives in therapy in their adulthood but this sense of having experienced trauma on their own, and the impact on their sense of self and alienation, remained even later in their fifties when they were engaging in therapy.

We also have had experiences of supervising other clinicians, and we could also all relate to the impact of vicarious trauma (trauma that results from listening to narratives of traumatic experiences). In line with this we have different narratives of supporting psychologists, and other healthcare professionals who after listening for many years to cases of child sexual abuse, presented with abnormal uterine bleeding. This presented as bleeding between monthly periods and experiencing prolonged bleeding.

In a diverse range of professionals who have presented to us following prolonged periods of trauma work in which they listened to or worked with psychological and physical abuse, sexual assault or abuse, a significant number also presented with medically unexplained symptoms or medically unexplained chronic pain in different parts of the body. These experiences from our practice begin to exemplify the impact that trauma has on not only the human psyche, but also its interconnectedness with physical health. Furthermore, it highlights that no one is immune to the impact of trauma, whether they are a child, adult or a health professional supporting those presenting with trauma. We have learnt that nothing in relation to trauma happens in isolation and that manifestation of trauma is a combination of all these factors; this view is a good way conceptualise trauma.

In line with conceptualisation of trauma, we often ask the client/patient to describe what they make of their experience of trauma. In discussing this, one of us shared how a friend had said that in society some communities talk about lucky people and unlucky people. The argument put forward was that actually the way you can tell if somebody is a 'lucky person' or an 'unlucky person' is to ask them their answer to the following scenario.

> So, you go into a bank and a robber comes in and he fires his gun and it hits you in the arm – what do you make of that? Are you unlucky or are you lucky?

There are different ways of responding. Those who see themselves as lucky may respond with: I am so lucky, that it was just my arm… it could have been my head, … now I can sell my story to the journalist and make some money out of it, etc. Those who conceptualise the event as unlucky could respond with how terrible that they were there at that time and their whole life has now changed, etc.

The thesis from this scenario argues that in some ways we create our own determinants of how we respond to traumatic experiences and that, through the ways in which we learn to respond to adversity from our primary care givers in our early years, we are prepared to be have a 'lucky outlook'. In more psychological terms, we would argue that our relational patterns and capacity for emotional regulation in the face of adversity or trauma is informed by the nature of attachments and relationships we have with primary care givers. If we have experiences in which we have a secure attachment and trust our primary care giver, then we inadvertently learn to trust ourselves and to trust others in relationships in the future. Thus, we could argue that attachment theory in relation to trauma suggests not just a pattern of relating to others but an expectation of how others are going to relate to you, and that if attachment has not been secure or good enough for the individual they will not expect that other people are going to be so. Furthermore, they may then not see opportunities for relational connections that are nurturing (and this may be as a result of having particular cognitive structures and worldviews that then perpetuate how you live in the world and recover/ find it difficult to recover from adversity).

These perspectives are the bedrock of the rise and importance of relational therapy interventions which focus specifically on addressing emotional dysregulation, critical thinking and challenge, self-compassion focused therapies, psychodynamic relational therapy for trauma, humanistic-existential therapies and transpersonal. While this list is not exhaustive, these therapies offer a perspective that trauma could be seen as something to learn from and that through, for example, making meaning from it, or identifying patterns that repeat, or challenging the way we think or learning to regulate our emotions, we can work through the trauma.

In relation to the cases we are about to now present, it is important that we illuminate and invite the reader to consider the significance of trauma across the lifespan as well as the importance of the politico-social-economic and environmental status as well as the belief systems of the individual and how these influence their trauma. It is also important to reflect on the support that these factors may contribute in buffering against trauma and re traumatisation.

Trauma across the lifespan – a presentation of three cases

Case 1

Case study of the person

Farrokh is a 38-year-old man from Western Asia. He describes himself as being a man from an ethnic minority background within his country of origin. He arrived in the UK seeking asylum 8 years ago. He shared a narrative of having arrived in the UK under a truck, having made a perilous journey fleeing from his home country, after escaping from prison where he had been arrested for 'political crimes'.

Family context

He stated that prior to being arrested he had been a happy family man, married with four daughters. He became interested in challenging injustice and was part of an activist group that was advocating for the rights of young women. This was something he felt was so important as he has daughters himself. He described being arrested at a peaceful protest and experienced arbitrary detention, torture and ill-treatment which he described in detail. At one point he described how through the night he would hear the cries and loud screams of men being beaten or tortured. He described that he was raped many times by the prison authorities and punished for what they said was an uprising against authority. Following serious injury, he was transferred to a hospital wing from where his escape was facilitated by a man who had compassion on him. He left his home country and over the next few days escaped without ever bidding his family farewell.

Social context

Furthermore, he stated that on arrival in the UK he constantly received racist abuse following the Brexit Referendum in 2016 and would often hear people shouting at him, 'Go back where you came back from.... You are not welcome here!!'. He stated that he has been struggling with a term he has heard in mainstream public discussion – 'hostile environment' – a term which was announced by the government in 2012 as intending 'to create here in Britain a really hostile environment for illegal immigration'.

The current protests in his home country which have been televised on BBC news (December 2022) triggered flashbacks, sleepless nights and serious psychological distress. Despite having been found by the police when they stopped a truck that was carrying him and few others, his asylum claim failed on the basis of not having any evidence for what happened to him and not remembering the exact dates of when he was tortured.

His psychological presentation includes flashbacks, nightmares, repetitive and distressing images and sensations of torture, body pain and aching, and often feeling sick. He describes being extremely anxious and feeling depressed.

Case 2

Case study of the person

Little V had two younger sisters and an older brother. Her father had died in a drunken accident when she was four; this shattered their mother and the family functioning, as their mother withdrew into a withdrawn depressed state, occasionally anaesthetising with street drugs.

Her older brother T joined the Navy as soon as he could, leaving the home and 10-year-old V as a surrogate mother to their sisters and mother. Shortly afterwards, her mother's drug dealer started to groom V. He introduced increasing threats of abuse to her sisters, and simultaneously, the opportunity to protect her sisters by engaging in sexual acts with him.

Over time V came to believe that she was choosing to perform sexual acts; she learned that if she initiated this as soon as he visited, she was able to distract him from frightening her sisters and the violence to her was reduced. She also learned (from her love of books) that if she became a character, the story stayed closed just as the door was closed as he left.

The character became more elaborated over the next three years and more distinct from her. Sometimes, when distressing memories opened, V learned that hurting herself seemed to somehow close the door again. This was another something that no one needed to know.

When the dealer was killed in a turf dispute, V was able to take this functioning self out into the world to college, along with her other traumatised self. Finding herself in a supportive environment she flourished, achieving good grades (she had always loved being absorbed in a book). At the local university she studied childcare and developmental psychology, and she met Sam, a potential partner. Sam was funny, kind and open and unlike anyone she had ever met. Their relationship slowly developed to intimacy, eventually initiated by Sam.

V and Sam, became aware that V was not herself during or after sex. She ran to the bathroom, locked the door and found something sharp. V was taken to A&E unconscious through loss of blood, required transfusion and was assessed by the liaison psychiatrist.

Case study 3

Case study of the person

Willow is 15 years old. She lives with her mother and stepfather.

Willow is a sensitive person, who prefers to be on her own. She doesn't like noisy environments and hates the fact that her stepfather has the television on at full volume, which she can hear from her bedroom.

Willow always tries to please her mother, but nothing she does ever seems to be good enough. Her mother expects her to help with the chores and babysit for her younger brother when she is at work.

Willow was never a big eater and when she was 14 years old she restricted her eating to the extent that she lost a lot of weight and her periods stopped.

After school Willow likes to listen to KPop music. She is obsessed by listening to the music, reading about the groups and following them on social media.

Family context

Willow's parents separated when she was only 3 years old. Her mum spoke about how abusive Willow's dad had been, although Willow doesn't remember him at all. She hasn't heard from him since he left. Willow's stepfather moved in a year later and shortly after that her younger brother was born.

Willow spent a lot of time with her maternal grandma. She often spent weekends with her grandma – her house was quiet and they would spend time doing activities like cooking and drawing together. When Willow was 10 years old, she was devastated when her grandma suddenly had a stroke and died a week later.

Social context

When Willow went to school at the age of 4 years (she was the youngest in her school year) she found the separation from her mother really difficult. She struggled to settle in at school and to make new friends, although she did like the school work.

Willow later found the transition to secondary school really difficult as the school was so much larger than her primary school. She started to 'act out' in class and often got sent out of the classroom.

Willow has one friend, India, who she spends a lot of time with. India also likes KPop music and wants to do everything with Willow, which Willow finds overwhelming at times.

In presenting these cases in this chapter, and throughout this book, we would like to invite you the reader to remain curious and to have an open mind about how you may conceptualise each individual's trauma. It is important to think about the individual person, and the wider context in which they live. We would also like to invite you to think about your own work and the challenges that those you work with may experience and how this impacts their lived experiences.

Reflection point 4.1

1 How might an understanding of trauma from the different cases be conceptualised from your approach or modality of training?
2 What may need to be considered in each of the cases in order to ensure a holistic assessment and therapeutic support?
3 What might you find challenging in working with each of the individuals presented?

5 Research in trauma

*Divine Charura, Emma Bradshaw
and Mark McFetridge*

Overview

- This chapter will outline some contemporary research findings on different interventions for trauma, as well as for racial trauma and intergenerational trauma.
- This will include findings from randomised controlled trials, and meta-analyses of research on cognitive behavioural therapy for trauma, eye movement desensitisation and reprocessing, cognitive processing therapy, cognitive therapy, prolonged exposure and present centred therapy.
- A unique aspect of this chapter will be its capacity to stimulate thought regarding assessments for trauma and relating to the societal level of trauma. Considerations for interventions for racial trauma and intergenerational trauma are also presented.

Introduction

The aims of this chapter are for the reader to engage with the research evidence base for trauma interventions and develop an understanding as well as critique of the current frontiers of knowledge within specific areas that we have chosen to focus on.

These include working with trauma on both an individual level as well as at a societal level. We therefore consider research findings and perspectives on treatments and interventions for embodied trauma, as well as for racial trauma and intergenerational trauma. We will make a case for, and provide examples of creative, critical methodologies within trauma research. One of the challenges of writing a chapter on research within the field of trauma is that, by the time the book is published, often the research may be outdated as research findings are constantly shifting the terrain of evidence. We value both practice-based evidence as well as evidence-based practice, and thus this chapter offers and critiques an array of findings.

As far back as 1927 Freud stated in 'The question of lay analysis':

> *In psycho-analysis there has existed from the very first an inseparable bond between cure and research. Knowledge brought therapeutic success. It was impossible to treat a patient without learning something new.* (1927: 255)

While Freud was writing specifically about psychoanalysis at the time (Freud, 1927), we assert that from our review of literature, and from our discussions relating to our own clinical practice, the sentiment of learning something new in all our encounters with those presenting with trauma remains true today. We have therefore written this chapter in a way that outlines themes and perspectives from the research we have reviewed rather than to conduct a systematic or scoping review.

We concur with Mills (2022) who argued that trauma has become an ordinary word used to describe everything from 'discretely aversive events to dissociative phenomena, prolonged psychic injury, attachment dysfunction, developmental arrest, and heinous acts against humanity' (p.1). Psychotraumatology research has profoundly influenced contemporary psychology and psychotherapy practice, as well as our understanding of history and the transgenerational transmission of trauma. This chapter focuses on some of the contemporary challenges in working with trauma, including embodied trauma and racial trauma. Research into the experience of trauma is dynamic and links closely to issues faced not only at an individual level, but at a societal one as well.

Do different traumatic events invoke different kinds of post-traumatic stress symptoms?

We agreed in our writing of this book that there are individual differences in reactions to traumatic events. Within the field of trauma there remain numerous discussions and debates on whether different traumatic events invoke different kinds of post-traumatic stress symptoms. Current research and developments have focused on the identification of a specific symptom profile of survivors of interpersonal and non-interpersonal trauma, and this has highlighted the importance of examining changes in differences in the symptom profile over time (Forbes et al., 2012). In line with this for example, Jaffe et al. (2019) presented evidence from cross-sectional and longitudinal studies evidence suggesting that PTSD symptoms that follow interpersonal trauma may increase the risk for later interpersonal trauma or in some cases secondary sexual victimisation (Gidycz, 2011). Put simply, this perspective posits that if an individual has had interpersonal trauma, such as adverse childhood experiences, and these are not processed (i.e. through therapy or other supportive relationships) they are likely to experience PTSD symptoms if they if they have a traumatic experience later in life. Furthermore, if they then develop PTSD symptoms in addition to a history of trauma, this further increases the risk for later interpersonal trauma.

Others have supported this perspective and concur that the experience of any past interpersonal trauma (i.e. physical abuse, emotional abuse, adverse childhood experiences or sexual assault) increased risk for a subsequent interpersonal trauma (Jaffe et al., 2019). As noted in research by Cougle et al. (2013), future predictions, from a number of baseline PTSD re-experiencing symptoms, rape history and history of childhood physical assault were all found to predict PTSD chronicity in the sample of women in the study two years later. Furthermore, chronic cases were also noted to more likely experience subsequent exposure to potentially traumatic stressors not involving interpersonal violence (Cougle et al., 2013).

PTSD symptoms are not always the most important mechanism through which trauma earlier in one's life increases the risk for post-traumatic stress or indeed complex trauma if one faces trauma later in life (Charura & Smith, 2023; Klest, 2012). When both PTSD symptoms and maladaptive post-traumatic cognitions are considered simultaneously, thoughts on the threat of harm emerge as the only unique factor that accounts for the association between past and subsequent interpersonal trauma. Where PTSD was initially described as resulting from a one-time severe traumatic or horrific incident, it is now widely accepted that it can be triggered by chronic multiple traumas as well (van der Kolk, 2000). In reviewing research literature on the nature of PTSD and trauma, and when comparing, having experienced trauma versus not experiencing interpersonal trauma, we note that individuals who have traumatic experiences often present with heightened concerns about threat, perceptions of danger and symptoms that evidence cognitions of fear and threat. This increased and continual hyperarousal over time, when faced with other traumas becomes one of the major contributors to PTSD and complex PTSD. In considering this question of whether different traumatic events invoke different kinds of post-traumatic stress symptoms, it is important to consider the role that other factors and variables play; for example, how an individual's environmental and social factors influence the risk of revictimisation is elevated in communities of low socioeconomic status (Klest, 2012).

Reflection point 5.1 – Modalities, approaches and interventions for working with trauma

1 What modalities, approaches and interventions for working with trauma are you familiar with?
2 What are your modalities and approaches of choice?
3 What is the latest research on these modalities that you aware of at present?

Diversity of modalities for working with trauma and PTSD

In this section we will now briefly outline some key findings from research we have found useful in our practice. There is a plethora of research on interventions for psychological trauma emerging from several fields relating to primary uni-modal approaches recommended for PTSD and complex PTSD. It is impossible for us to review all the research in this chapter, therefore our aim in this section is to point the reader to the diversity of research available on modalities and interventions, some of which we have drawn from meta-analyses and randomised controlled trials (RCTs). The research we reviewed, for example, includes that conducted by Lewis et al. (2020) whose systematic review and meta-analysis reviewed 114 randomised controlled trials (RCTs) and included 8171 partici-pants. The evidence they presented showed that there was robust evidence that the therapies broadly defined as CBT with a trauma focus (CBT-T), as well as eye movement desensitisation and reprocessing (EMDR), had a clinically important effect. Their findings showed that manualised CBT-Ts with the strongest evi-dence of effect were cognitive processing therapy (CPT), cognitive therapy (CT) and prolonged exposure (PE). In addition they showed that there was also some evidence supporting CBT without a trauma focus, group CBT with a trauma focus, guided internet-based CBT and present centred therapy (PCT). Further-more, there was emerging evidence for a number of other therapies and they concluded that a recent increase in RCTs of psychological therapies for PTSD enabled them to give a more confident recommendation of CBT-T and EMDR as the first-line treatments among the CBT-Ts considered by the review (Lewis et al., 2020).

While this is the recommendation in relation to EMDR, it is worth also noting that there have been increasing studies on EMDR with different client groups presenting with trauma. A meta-analysis by Balkin et al. (2022) evaluated the comparative effectiveness of EMDR in the treatment of symptoms of over arousal and comparing effectiveness in the treatment of anxiety and post-trau-matic stress disorder (PTSD). Their results showed mixed findings and they suggested that although their findings showed that EMDR may be beneficial, there is an equivalent chance that future applications with similar samples could result in findings regarded as considerably or categorically ineffective (Balkin et al., 2022). They pointed to numerous limitations including noting that the actual effect of the bilateral stimulation used in EMDR continues to be unknown, with few studies on record comparing the processing of trauma with-out bilateral stimulation to EMDR with bilateral stimulation. They also noted that 'based upon Shapiro's (1989) acknowledgement on the development of EMDR, the extent to which eye movement, as a mechanism of change within the adaptive information processing model is associated with the decrease in over-arousal continues to be suspect' (Balkin et al., 2022, p.120).

In a systematic review and meta-analysis of qualitative research of children and adolescents' experiences of trauma-focused cognitive behavioural ther-apy, results evidenced that trauma focused CBT (tf-CBT) showed large improvements across all outcomes from pre- to post-treatment and favourable results compared to any control condition including wait-list, treatment as usual and active treatment at post-treatment (Thielemann et al., 2022). Other research focuses on CPT and results suggesting that CPT can be effectively implemented in its various forms to a broad range of patients (Graziano et al., 2023; Roberge et al., 2022).

Other modalities such as narrative exposure therapy (NET), in comparison with non-trauma-focused treatment in post-traumatic stress disorder, have also shown varying degrees of effectiveness (Grech & Grech, 2020). For example, one systematic review and meta-analysis of NET presented findings that showed that patients and clinicians may expect sustained treatment results from NET (Lely et al., 2019). It has been suggested, however, that more research is needed to further explore the benefits of NET for different populations and trauma-types (Grech & Grech, 2020). More is written about narrative exposure therapy in Chapter 10 in relation to working with different cultures.

There have also continued to be developments in different modalities in addition to these; for example, psychodynamic psychotherapy for post-traumatic stress disorder (Stiles et al., 2008). Some studies, for example, have considered the effect of psychodynamic therapy (PDT) on PTSD, noting that PDT enhanced patients' ability to resolve emotional reactions to trauma by increasing their reflective capacity (Levi, 2020). We have noted from reviewing the psychodynamic literature that research in this area focuses on the impact of trauma on the psyche and on ego function, and on specific imaginative and resource-oriented techniques. There has also been a plethora of emerging research on the effectiveness of interventions drawing on humanistic-existential principles which focus on reframing a new self-concept following trauma and developing the capacity for post-traumatic growth (Murphy et al., 2019).

Other research has included the work of van der Kolk et al. (2014) who conducted a randomised controlled study into trauma-informed yoga or supportive women's health education as an adjunctive treatment for post-traumatic stress disorder for women with chronic, treatment-resistant PTSD. Their results showed that both groups exhibited significant decreases in PTSD symptoms during the first half of treatment, but these improvements were maintained in the yoga group, while the control group relapsed after its initial improvement. Hence, yoga significantly reduced PTSD symptomatology, with effect sizes comparable to well-researched psychotherapeutic and psychopharmacologic approaches. It is noted that yoga may improve the functioning of individuals presenting with trauma by helping them to tolerate physical and sensory experiences associated with fear and helplessness and to increase emotional awareness and affect tolerance (Tan et al., 2023; van der Kolk, et al., 2014; Zaccari et al., 2023).

While these are only a very few systematic reviews, meta-analyses and findings from the research we outlined here, their conclusions for future research all point us to a summary of recommendations. Namely that these diverse interventions are effective in varying degrees in reducing PTSD symptoms, depression and anxiety in different populations, but that more studies with larger samples and better designs are needed. We also add that it is important that all research should engage with a decolonised approach (Charura & Lago, 2021b; Charura & Wicaksono, 2023) and the inclusivity of a diversity of clients from ethnically diverse populations.

Importance of research on embodied trauma

There is emerging research which is building on our understanding of how individuals' experiences of traumatic events contribute to the development of somatic symptoms.

Van der Kolk (2022) noted that their research showed that steady yoga practice for a traumatised person was more effective than any medication. He argued that the core issue is not 'what happened to you' but the fact that trauma gets stuck in the body. Furthermore, he went on to describe how in some of their research, on the immune systems of people presenting with trauma, they found that when people are traumatised their immune system starts overreacting and the body of the individual starts attacking itself; he argued that this is a good metaphor for people's bodies getting stuck in a state of terror (van der Kolk, 2022).

It has been long argued that these symptoms are the body's expression of deep psychological distress. They are a result of trauma becoming stuck in the body and the individual oscillating between states of hypo or hyper arousal, resulting in constant dysregulation of the autonomic nervous system (O'Brien & Charura, 2022, 2023).

A comprehensive literature scoping review by O'Brien and Charura (2022) on refugees, asylum seekers and practitioners' perspectives of embodied trauma highlights the need for a clear definition of terms and for the development of a culturally informed assessment and formulation for individuals experiencing embodied trauma. It also revealed a gap in the research for the best treatment approach(es) for embodied trauma. Through this scoping review they formulated a clear definition of embodied trauma and key themes for future research including the importance of culturally informed care, psychosocial support, language considerations, relational belonging and inclusion of sexual, spiritual and existential factors, moving away from purely Eurocentric diagnostic frameworks and treatments and more towards culturally informed care (O'Brien & Charura, 2022).

In developing research in this area their novel descriptions of embodied trauma we refer to, which we agreed is applicable to those presenting with embodied trauma, is that it is:

> *"... the whole body's response to a significant traumatic event, where mental distress is experienced within the body as a physiological, psychological, biological, cultural, or relational reaction to trauma. Embodied trauma may include psychosomatic symptoms alongside the inability to self-regulate the autonomic nervous system and emotions, resulting in states of dissociation, numbing, relational disconnection, changed perceptions or non-verbal internal experiences which affect every-day functioning."* (O'Brien & Charura, 2022)

In further developing their research in the areas of refugees and asylum seekers' perspectives of embodied trauma they presented a body mapping methodology as an innovative method for psychotraumatology research and practice. In this work, O'Brien and Charura referred to Caizzi (2012) who described trauma as becoming embodied in the subsymbolic mode and stated that this can include the sensory, somatic, affective and also motor modes of mental processing. She argued that a traumatic experience in adulthood deeply impacts and changes the protocol level of the victim's psychological script (Caizzi, 2012). Van der Kolk (2014) had highlighted that trauma can also be portrayed through non-verbal manifestations owing to the suppression of Broca's area of the brain, which is responsible for language resulting in trauma being mediated non-verbally through the body (van der Kolk, 2014). O'Brien and Charura (2023) asserted that if trauma research in the psychological therapies is going to be impactful, effective and authentic within our contemporary and diverse world, then it is important that trauma be addressed at both its conscious and unconscious levels. This includes in its portrayal in dissociative experiences as a type of verbal and non-verbal 'body language' (Arizmendi, 2008: 443). We concur with O'Brien and Charura (2023) about a trajectory in which trauma researchers and practitioners continue maintaining an open and curious stance about engaging with embodied trauma creatively across cultural expressions and contexts.

Centrality of the therapeutic relationship, and not just trauma therapeutic interventions

Reflection point 5.2 – Challenges in the therapeutic relationship
What challenges have you faced, or do you think a therapist may face, in working with clients presenting with trauma?

The contemporary body of literature and research primarily argues that longer-term work with clients presenting with trauma requires deeper therapeutic relationships and trust for the client to feel safe, contained and psychologically held to enable them to process their trauma (Charura & Smith, 2023; Dyer & Corrigan, 2021; Lord, 2019). Paul and Haugh (2008) reminded us about the potency of the therapeutic relationship, and they asserted that 'the importance of the therapeutic relationship in research should not be underestimated' (Paul & Haugh, 2008, p. 10). They referred to a metanalysis of research by Orlinsky et al. (1994) who noted the power of the therapeutic relationship as reflected in over one thousand studies. In this they reflected key criteria, which we believe are applicable to trauma work too, and these included therapist credibility, skill, collaborativeness, empathic understanding, affirmation of the client and attention to the client's affective experience as associated with positive outcomes (Paul & Haugh, 2008). Furthermore, it is noted that the most important determinants of therapeutic outcomes include:

1 The quality of the client's participation in therapy as the most important determinant.
2 The therapeutic bond, especially as determined by the client.
3 The therapist's contribution, especially through 'empathic, affirmative, collaborative and self-congruent engagement' (Orlinsky et al., 1994: 361) with the client.
4 The skilful application of potent interventions (in the context of trauma research, we assert that this includes practice-based evidenced interventions and those with an evidence base drawn from research).

We have also been drawn to the approach of Murphy et al. (2019) which identifies and provides a new method for establishing person-centred experiential therapy principles for early trauma-focused work. They presented four trauma-focused therapist principles which they identified as important. These include:

a) supporting early relationship building/alliance formation
b) facilitating client identification and recognition of past events as trauma experiences
c) facilitating work on traumatic sources of current experiential and interpersonal difficulties
d) offering self agency focused empathy.

Having identified the primacy of the therapeutic relationship in this way, the section that follows identifies findings from research regarding facilitating and conducting psychological assessments.

Research and guidelines on facilitating trauma assessments

Sweeney et al. (2021) completed research funded by the National Institute for Health Research (NIHR) which resulted in them formulating evidence-based guidelines for conducting trauma-informed talking therapy assessments. We highlight these guidelines in this chapter as they are based on robust, survivor-led research that builds on existing good practice in the field. Rather than focusing on the technical aspects and skill base of how to conduct assessments, or how to ask about trauma experiences (Ferentz, 2018; Kisiel et al., 2021; Read et al., 2007), the guidelines we refer to were formulated to integrate trauma-informed practice into assessment processes for a diversity of modalities. The key aim is to understanding trauma and how it impacts on people. Thus, the recommendation we give is of taking a trajectory in your practice that moves away from assessment processes and therapeutic support that is bureaucratic and leans more towards a compassionate, humanised and culturally appropriate approach (O'Brien & Charura, 2023; Sweeney et al., 2021). The key recommendations from the research by Sweeney et al. (2021) we note here include:

- Assessment processes should be co-developed and co-produced by trauma survivors and services supporting them. Co-production of trauma-informed approaches help to ensure that needs and experiences are placed at the centre of service design and delivery.
- A recommendation for an initial meeting rather than an assessment can facilitate better assessment processes, including people not then having to undergo assessments for service provision they are not eligible for. We have noted in our own work the frustration that many survivors and clients voice because of having to retell their narrative and traumatic experiences, even in cases where they then are told they are not eligible for the service.
- The importance of therapists using their power positively to enable those they work with and support. In line with this it has been suggested that it is important to acknowledge the existence of an inherent power differential between researchers and participants. Power with clients presenting with trauma, rather than power over them, allows for a collaborative, formulation-driven approach, thereby enabling an understanding of each individual's own personal meaning-making about the causation and impact of their experiences of trauma (O'Brien & Charura, 2022, 2023; Proctor, 2021).
- Part of what is key in managing one's power is through the therapists understanding a range of things. These include historical, structural and social traumas such as racism, homophobia, poverty, the legacy of slavery and other wider systemic contexts in which clients' traumatic experiences may have originated or perpetuated.
- Furthermore, research highlights that successful assessments were those in which therapists recognised and valued the expertise that people presenting with trauma bring and offered support in ways that foregrounded safety and flexibility.
- It was also noted that successful assessments were those in which therapists listened, communicated their compassion as well as humanity to the client, experienced as authentic, and in which they prioritised building trust, avoided pathologising language and demonstrated empathy.

We acknowledge that the list of recommendations given here is not exhaustive, and that some areas will continually require substantial further exploration in the context of individual practice and wider services. Furthermore, we also note that in most research reviewed in the writing of this book and from our experience in practice, it is important for therapists to recognise the signs of burnout and/or vicarious trauma and take appropriate action. Such action includes reflection, self-care and appropriate supervision as well as services ensuring that referrals to specialist trauma services (including women's organisations, or survivor-led organisations for minoritised groups) are facilitated where people want them (Sweeney et al., 2021).

Other research which has focused on the therapeutic relationship includes a metasynthesis of 23 published case studies of patients with functional somatic syndromes (FSS) from various psychotherapeutic orientations by Krivzov et al. (2021). In their research they examined interpersonal dynamics and the therapeutic relationship in patients with FSS (Krivzov et al., 2021). They argued that clients presenting with FSS often engage in ways that portray maladaptive interpersonal patterns in the therapeutic relationship, including perceiving others as unreliable, that is, unavailable, overcontrolling and overprotective; some consequently drop out of therapy. Their research highlights the importance of practitioners offering a more interpersonal perspective on emotion regulation difficulties and challenges in interpersonal dynamics. This is especially important when working with those whose creative adjustments because of their trauma include pleasing others, controlling others or emotional avoidance. We concur with Krivzov et al. (2021) who from a methodological perspective stated that as functional somatic symptoms relating to trauma cannot be understood sufficiently by quantitative methods alone, there is a need for in-depth qualitative research.

Trauma work at societal level: what the research is telling us

---

Reflection point 5.3 – Working with trauma at a societal level

1 What modalities, approaches and interventions for working with trauma at a societal level are you familiar with?
2 Which groups in society do you think may need interventions for trauma at a community or societal level?

Research into the experience of trauma is dynamic and links closely to issues faced not only at an individual level but at a societal one as well. The UK Psychological Trauma Society (UKPTS, 2022) refers to research into important issues such as climate change, disasters and collective trauma, all of which have been the focus of recent research in the trauma field. It continues to be important to address trauma and its impacts at a societal level. For example, climate change is of major global concern and its psychological impact is increasingly being considered too. A recent systematic literature review conducted by Vecchio et al. (2022) highlighted the impact of cumulative changes in climate on the mental health of indigenous peoples. In such research there is increasing acknowledgement that acute weather events can impact people at both an individual level (e.g. mental wellbeing due to grief, loss of possessions and PTSD) and a societal level (e.g. social environment or displacement) which demonstrates the importance of ongoing research in this area. As the occurrence of disasters is likely to increase in upcoming years, factors such as developing societal resilience are important to consider as well as engaging with indigenous communities in responding to climate change. Furthermore, it is important to take a collaborative approach with indigenous communities in formulating interventions for mental health challenges arising from the impact of climate change (Cappelli et al., 2021).

Racial trauma and intergenerational trauma are also other areas in which we have focused as they impact not only individuals but whole communities and societies.

Research on treatments for racial trauma and complex racial trauma

In the writing of this book, we engaged in numerous conversations about our experiences of working with clients from ethnically diverse communities and the devastating impact of racial trauma that we have witnessed. Furthermore, during the writing of this book, we engaged with the increasing voices who rightly spoke against the murder of Mr George Floyd and the heightened awareness within the therapy professions on the importance of social justice (Cooper, 2023; Oulanova et al., 2023; Smith et al., 2021; Winter, 2019; Winter & Charura, 2023). This increased awareness, however, builds on decades of research and literature which highlighted how North American, European and colonial zeitgeist societies, Black, indigenous, and people of colour (BIPOC) [the global majority], experience racial microaggressions and interpersonal, institutional and systemic racism on a repetitive, constant, inevitable and cumulative basis (Alleyne, 2011; Cénat, 2023; Charura & Lago, 2021a; Lago & Hirai, 2013; Lago, 2006). Despite literature and research that asserts the impact of microaggressions, institutional and systemic racism, there remains a paucity of research on racial trauma. Given the potential impact as well as lived experience of the global majority, we decided to focus on research on racial trauma.

Racial trauma refers to the events of danger related to real or perceived experience of racial discrimination, threats of harm and injury, as well as humiliating or shaming events, in addition to witnessing harm to other ethnoracial individuals because of real or perceived racism (Butts, 2002;

Cénat, 2023). Chavez-Dueñas et al. (2019) defined ethno-racial trauma as the individual and/or collective psychological distress and fear of danger that results from experiencing or witnessing discrimination, threats of harm, violence and intimidation directed at ethno-racial minority groups (Chavez-Dueñas et al., 2019). It has been noted that race-based traumatic stress trauma differs from post-traumatic stress disorder (PTSD) in that victims are exposed to constant racial microaggressions and that racial trauma has significant effects on mental and physical health as well as on social and economic aspects of victims' lives (Cénat, 2023). Butts (2002) critiqued the DSM for its failure to account for racial discrimination as a potentially traumatising event and, thus, its failure to capture the potential for racial discrimination to result in PTSD. Although the scientific literature has become more focused on race-based trauma, few studies have been devoted to culturally sensitive treatments that can adequately address racial trauma and its impact. There are however some attempts to develop treatments for racial trauma as well as to highlight research on racial trauma (Bryant-Davis & Ocampo, 2005; Chavez-Dueñas et al., 2019; Chioneso et al., 2020; Comas-Díaz, 2016; Markin & Coleman, 2023; Metzger et al., 2021).

Findings by Comas-Díaz (2016) in an empirical study on the perceived racial discrimination among African Americans, Latina/os, and Asian Americans suggested that racism may be a traumatic experience. Their research was based on a design of a race-informed therapeutic approach that integrated systems of ethnic healing, liberation psychology and culturally appropriate traditional therapies to address racial trauma. They noted that psychological treatment of racial trauma victims is needed, and that it can be achieved through empowering survivors to render themselves more capable of expressing and transforming their reality. Consequently, they argued that most therapists ignore racial trauma and the clients' racial wounds, thus it is imperative that action is taken by clinicians to urgently address these issues in treatment (Comas-Díaz, 2016).

Chavez-Dueñas et al. (2019) through their research also presented a framework to stimulate healing from ethno-racial trauma. They entitled their four-phase framework HEART (Healing Ethno And Racial Trauma). Grounded in the principles of liberation psychology and trauma-informed care, the framework is composed of four phases. These include: establishing sanctuary spaces for Latinx [those from ethnically diverse or minority groups] experiencing ethnoracial trauma; acknowledging, reprocessing and coping with symptoms of ethnoracial trauma; strengthening and connecting individuals, families and communities to survival strategies and cultural traditions that heal; empowering individuals and communities for liberation and resistance (Chavez- Dueñas et al., 2019).

Chioneso et al. (2020) identified three major components of a framework for working with racial trauma. This included: (a) justice as both a condition of and an outcome of healing on a community level; (b) culturally syntonic processes (i.e., storytelling and resistance) and that these can direct the renarrating of trauma and act as conduits for transformation; (c) psychological dimensions that promote justice-informed outcomes (examples of these include connectedness, collective memory and critical consciousness) (Chioneso et al., 2020).

Others (like Metzger et al., 2021) conducted research on healing interpersonal and racial trauma and the integration of racial socialisation into trauma-focused cognitive behavioural therapy with African-American youth. In their research they utilised the racial encounter coping appraisal and socialisation theory to propose suggestions for adapting trauma-focused cognitive behavioural therapy as an evidence-based trauma treatment for children and adolescents. It included racial socialisation as a process of transmitting culture, attitudes and values to help youth overcome stressors associated with ethnic minority status (Metzger et al., 2021).

Williams et al. (2021) completed a review of literature on the evidence of harms in relation to racism and how it has been linked to a host of negative mental health conditions, and the connection between racial discrimination and PTSD symptoms (Williams et al., 2021). Furthermore, they outlined research which focuses on the mechanisms of race-related stress or trauma responses, which may be salient in terms of traumatisation; they also highlighted numerous studies which outlined findings on assessment, treatment from a diversity of modalities and they also noted future directions.

Other research has focused on the intersections of gendered racial trauma and childbirth trauma in Black women. Markin and Coleman (2023) highlighted how Black women, in particular, were three to four times more likely to experience dangerous and even life-threatening complications. Furthermore, they noted that Black women were more likely to report mistreatment and neglect from medical providers and staff during childbirth. They argued that the experiences with gendered racism during childbirth (which in itself is a vulnerable, intense and potentially traumatic experience when proper support is absent), may lead to post-traumatic stress reactions. In this research they asserted that psychotherapy for racial trauma can help affected women to process gendered racial and childbirth traumas through: (a) the establishment of a safe, trusting and collaborative therapeutic relationship, in which careful attention is given to repairing therapeutic ruptures caused by cultural misunderstandings or gendered racial microaggressions; and (b) framing experiences and 'symptoms' as understandable reactions to gendered race-based traumatic stress during childbirth (Markin & Coleman, 2023).

We concur with Cénat (2023), who offered through her research guidelines for assessment and treatment for complex racial trauma. She rightly noted that 'similar to complex trauma, racial trauma surrounds the victims' life course and engenders consequences on their physical and mental health, behavior, cognition, relationships with others, self-concept, and social and economic life' (Cénat, 2023, p. 695). She argued that there is no way to identify racial trauma other than through a life-course approach that captures the complex nature of individual, collective, historical and intergenerational experiences of racism and trauma experienced by global majority communities in Western society (Cénat, 2023).

The research we have reviewed here to varying degrees all asserts that there is still much work to be done to address the reality of racial trauma and that the next critical steps include raising awareness of racial trauma among clinicians. This includes incorporating the assessment and treatment of racial trauma into clinical training programs. It is also noted that instruments that consider the different aspects of racial trauma (repetitive, constant, collective/cumulative, inevitable, etc.) are needed. Similarly, recommendations for future research also highlights a critical need to develop appropriate treatments as well as to evaluate their efficacy. Moreover, there is an increasing call for adding some discussion and inclusion of racial trauma in important diagnostic manuals such as the DSM-5 (Williams et al., 2021) while others have made a call for a critique on whether diagnostic manuals are the right framework as opposed to use of other frameworks, such as the power threat meaning framework (Charura & Al-Murri, forthcoming).

Research on inter/transgenerational trauma and rethinking historical trauma

In our discussions in writing this book, we explored the diversity critique that has been raised against the concept of intergenerational trauma and the challenges in researching this aspect of trauma. For example, Braga et al. (2012) argued that literature on the transgenerational transmission of trauma shows mixed findings regarding this subject and that although some clinical studies reported psychopathological findings related to transgenerational transmission of trauma, some empirical research conversely found no evidence of this phenomenon in offspring of Holocaust survivors. Having noted this, however, in our recent review of literature we noted a systematic review by Dashorst et al. (2019) on the intergenerational consequences of the Holocaust on the mental health of offspring. In their systematic review they identified 23 eligible studies published between 2000 and 2018. They noted that various parent and child characteristics and their interaction were found to contribute to the development of psychological symptoms and biological and epigenetic variations. Furthermore, there was evidence suggesting that Holocaust survivor offspring showed a heightened vulnerability for stress, although this was only evident in the face of actual danger. Finally, the results also evidenced intergenerational effects on offspring cortisol levels (Dashorst et al., 2019).

The following quote encapsulates for us why continued research in this area is important. Kirmayer et al. (2014, p. 313) noted:

> *The recognition that the violence and suffering experienced by one generation can have effects on subsequent generations provides an important insight into the origins of mental health problems. However, the kinds of adversity faced by each generation differ, and the construct of trauma does not capture many of the important elements that are rooted in structural problems, including poverty and discrimination.*

We concur with the conclusion by Kirmayer et al. (2014) that it is important in understanding the ways in which trauma impacts mental health by taking a broader view of identity, community, adaptation and resistance as forms of resilience. We explore and discuss this perspective further later in the book (see Chapter 11 on transcultural perspectives to working with trauma).

Another model we noted from trauma research is the conceptual framework of historical trauma developed by Hartmann et al. (2019). It can be best understood through the collective experience of historical oppressions that result in cumulative effects with cross-generational impacts. This framework, although based on a review of studies with American-Indian populations, remains important as it was intended to achieve recognition for the ongoing impacts of historical violence, such as the Holocaust, other genocides or settler colonialism, on the lives of subsequent generations. Its main recommendations emphasised aspects that are key in therapeutic relationships when working from a transcultural perspective with those experiencing trauma (Hartmann et al., 2019). These include:

1 Clarifying clinical concepts (e.g. clinical syndrome versus the clients relaying their idioms of distress)
2 Disentangling clinical narratives of individual pathology (e.g., trauma and complex trauma) from social narratives of population adversity (e.g. survivance stories)
3 Attending to features of settler-colonialism not easily captured by health indices (e.g. structural violence and systemic racism oppression etc.)
4 Encouraging alignment of anticolonial efforts, decolonising trauma practice with constructive critiques establishing conceptual bridges to disciplines that can help to advance psychological understandings of colonisation and indigenous wellness (e.g. postcolonial studies, transcultural trauma psychology and going beyond decolonisation by seeing other epistemologies which are non-Eurocentric as equal knowledge-generating partners in psychotraumatology research and practice) (Hartmann et al., 2019).

We note that, for example, African psychology, Islamic psychology, Eastern psychology bodies of knowledge and so on, are influential in their own right in conceptualising formulations of how trauma is understood in different cultures and trauma can be treated. As such, some clients we work with may have understanding of trauma that is different to how practitioners drawing from the DSM-V, or ICD-11, psychodynamic diagnostic taxonomies or other Eurocentric orientated modalities may conceptualise and formulate experiences of trauma or complex trauma. In line with this we highlight the limitations of research voices and evidence from non-Eurocentric epistemologies. As we value a decolonised approach to trauma we have continually appreciated frameworks and modalities that highlight ways of working with embodied trauma, religion and spirituality, and in ways that evidence decolonised and culturally appropriate and sensitive approaches (Charura & Lago, 2021a, 2021b; Lago & Charura, 2015; Lago & Hirai, 2013; O'Brien & Charura, 2022, 2023).

Conclusion

This chapter focuses on some of the contemporary challenges in working with trauma. Presenting research on different modalities has highlighted both the effectiveness of these different interventions to varying degrees in reducing a diversity of trauma PTSD symptoms, in different populations. Drawing from our interest of working with trauma on a societal level we have also focused not only on trauma at the individual level but considered research findings and perspectives on treatments and interventions for racial trauma and intergenerational trauma. Our conclusion, however, is clear. There remains a need for more studies with larger samples and better designs. In the spirit of this book which is about inclusivity we have also argued that all research within the field of psychotraumatology should engage with decolonised approaches and the inclusion of a diversity of clients from ethnically diverse populations.

Reflection point 5.4 – Working with trauma at a societal level

1 Reflect on your practice, and on the recommendations noted in this chapter. What do you see as missing from your own practice?
2 What research do you need to develop more and how will you achieve this to become a practitioner whose work is informed by research evidence?

6

Psychopathology and complex trauma

Divine Charura, Mark McFetridge and Emma Bradshaw

Overview

- This chapter will consider psychopathology and complex trauma.
- We consider different diagnostic criteria for post-traumatic stress disorder (PTSD)
- We also emphasise the importance of conceptualising trauma as presented in the cases we discuss from non-pathologising frameworks including the power threat meaning framework, fragile process and moral injury lenses.

Introduction

This chapter illuminates our interest in human relationships, the motivation that humans have for contact with others and relationships and the manifestation of psychopathology in relation to trauma. In the last few decades, we have witnessed an extraordinary explosion of new theoretical perspectives in the trauma psychopathology literature, and this has contributed to our understanding of how trauma and complex trauma manifest across the human lifespan. Some of our theoretical conceptualisations of psychopathological manifestation of trauma and complex trauma will be exemplified, building on the cases presented in Chapter 4. In attempting to understand human relationships, the way humans develop their psyche and their bio-psycho-social-sexual-spiritual capacities (O'Brien & Charura, 2023), we demonstrate in this chapter how trauma can thwart these potentialities and their development and progress.

This chapter discusses the current diagnostic criteria for the core symptoms for post-traumatic stress disorder (PTSD) and complex PTSD (CPTSD) as noted in the *Diagnostic and Statistical Manual of Mental Disorders* (DSM-5) (2013), the *International Classification of Diseases* 11th Revision (ICD-11) and the criteria noted in the *Psychodynamic Diagnostic Manual* (PDM-2)

(2017) (American Psychiatric Association, 2013; Lingiardi & MacWilliams, 2017; World Health Organisation, 2022). We also present a critique of psychopathology, including PTSD, traumatic grief, dissociative states and moral injury, and consider the origins of the clinical term 'complex trauma' which only recently became a formal diagnosis within ICD-11 (WHO, 2022). Furthermore, the additional difficulties experienced by those with complex PTSD will be evaluated.

Our aim in this chapter is therefore to go beyond viewing the psychopathology of trauma from diagnostic taxonomies by also offering an alternative conceptual system and accessible relational perspectives on trauma or complex trauma presentations. These include understanding trauma through the lens of what has been termed 'difficult process', which is also known as 'fragile process', and dissociative processes (Warner, 2000, 2013); formulating PTSD presentations from a relational perspective (Charura & Smith, 2023) and trauma from a person-centred perspective (Hipólito et al., 2014). We also draw from the power threat meaning framework (Johnstone & Boyle, 2018) and critical perspectives which have been encapsulated as 'people not pathology' (Sanders & Tolan, 2023) and focus on cutting-edge examples of therapeutic work with trauma and applications to different and diverse groups within society. The resources and questions offered through this chapter help you the reader to engage with the theories and examples given while enabling you to reflect on your own learning and practice.

Psychopathology and complex trauma

There is a plethora of evidence that shows that by the time an individual reaches adolescence, they are likely to have experienced at least one traumatic event (Connell et al., 2018). Additionally, when compared to trauma in adulthood, exposure to traumatic experiences is at its peak during the adolescent years (Finkelhor et al., 2007). Further research has examined negative sequels associated with traumatic experiences and traumatic stress and has evidenced that there is a high prevalence of presentations such as anxiety, depression, behaviour disorders and PTSD among traumatised adolescents (Charura & Smith, 2023; Huh et al., 2017; Van Assche et al., 2020). Thus, we conclude that there is consistent demonstration within research evidence of the relationship between negative childhood experiences and the development of psychological difficulties in adulthood. As we have argued so far in this book, that trauma impacts the biological, psychological, social, sexual and spiritual domains of functioning (bio-psycho-social-sexual-spiritual) (O'Brien & Charura, 2022), we therefore maintain that central mechanisms to traumatic stress include alterations in physiological reactivity which are linked to adverse childhood environmental experiences. These physiological and environmental experiences contribute to the internalisation and externalisation of psychopathology. In line with this, Heleniak et al. (2016) argued that childhood trauma exposure may influence physiological reactivity to stress in distinct ways from other forms of childhood adverse childhood experiences (Heleniak et al., 2016).

What is post-traumatic stress disorder (PTSD)?

The diagnostic criteria for post-traumatic stress disorder were first officially defined in 1980 when the American Psychiatric Association published the third edition of the *Diagnostic and Statistical Manual of Mental Disorders* (DSM-III). In this section, rather than repeat the full criteria for PTSD and complex trauma as outlined in the DSM-5 and the *International Classification of Diseases* 11th Revision (ICD-11) we will focus on the core symptoms for PTSD and complex trauma common to both the ICD-11 (WHO, 2022) and the DSM-5 (APA, 2013) criteria. It is, however, important to note that although the concept of CPTSD is longstanding (Herman, 1992/2022), it is not in the fifth edition of the *Diagnostic and Statistical Manual of Mental Disorders* (DSM-5), and therefore is not officially recognised by the American Psychiatric Association (APA). However, it is listed in the *International Classification of Diseases* 11th Revision (ICD-11) by the World Health Organisation (2022) which contains major changes to the diagnosis of PTSD. It is replaced by two separate diagnoses: PTSD and CPTSD. According to the ICD-11, PTSD can be diagnosed if an individual was exposed to at least one traumatic life experience and meets the diagnostic criteria for PTSD (symptom clusters of re-experiencing, avoidance and sense of threat). The ICD-11 CPTSD could be diagnosed when, alongside all PTSD criteria, three additional symptom clusters called 'disturbances in self-organisation' or 'DSO' occur. These are, namely, affect dysregulation, negative self-concept and difficulties in relationships (WHO, 2022).

Box 6.1 Core symptoms of PTSD ICD 11-2022

Core Symptoms of PTSD
- Re-experiencing
- Avoidance
- Hyperarousal and reactivity.

Plus, disturbances in self-organisation (DSO):

- difficulty regulating emotions
- negative self-concept (such as feelings of guilt, shame and loneliness)
- interpersonal problems which impact on building and maintaining relationships.

It is important for us to state that not everyone who experiences traumatic events will then develop CPTSD. One explanation of this may be that interventions for trauma mitigate in some people the symptoms getting worse and developing into CPTSD.

In addition to the information in Table 6.1, which follows, we have also highlighted the summary of the PTSD Diagnostic. This is in line with the DSM-5 (APA, 2013) criteria applying to adults, adolescents and children older than 6 years.

Table 6.1 Summary of PTSD diagnostic criteria

PTSD (DSM-5, 2013)	PTSD (ICD-11, 2022)
A. **Exposure to actual or threatened death, serious injury, or sexual violence in one (or more ways)** i.e., direct exposure; witnessing trauma; learning that a relative or friend was exposed to trauma; experiencing repeated or extreme exposure to aversive details of trauma.	• Exposure to extremely threatening or horrific event or series of events.
B. **Re-experiencing of intrusive symptoms** i.e. distressing memories; nightmares; dissociative reactions such as flashbacks; or emotional or distress or physiologic reactivity after exposure to traumatic reminders.	• Re-experiencing • Avoidance • Persistent perceptions of heightened current threat.
C. **Avoidance of stimuli associated with the event** i.e. trauma-related thoughts or feelings or external reminders.	
D. **Negative changes in cognitions and mood that began or worsened after the trauma** i.e. memory loss; overly negative thoughts and assumptions about oneself or the world; exaggerated blame of self or others for causing the trauma; feeling isolated.	
E. **Alterations in arousal and reactivity that began or worsened after the trauma** i.e. irritable behaviour or aggression; reckless or destructive behaviour; hypervigilance; exaggerated startle response, difficulty concentrating; difficulty sleeping.	
F. **Duration.** Symptoms last for more than one month.	• Must last at least several weeks.
G. **Functional significance.** Symptoms cause clinically significant distress or functional impairment (e.g. social, occupational).	• Significant impairment in personal, family social educational, occupational or other important areas of social functioning.
H. **Exclusion.** Symptoms are not due to medication, substance misuse or other illness.	

Having presented a summary of the diagnostic criteria for PTSD, we acknowledge that the presentation of more complex responses to trauma have been argued to fit in a separate category of complex post-traumatic stress disorder (CPTSD) (Herman, 1992/2022). We concur that these types of traumatic experiences involve additional cognitive, emotional, behavioural, relational and characterological changes beyond the symptoms of PTSD, thereby implying a need for adapted models of understanding and treatment (Charura & Smith, 2023; Dyer & Corrigan, 2021; Karatzias et al., 2019). We advocate and highlight the importance of accessing the latest diagnostic manuals to familiarise yourself with the full criteria. At the time of writing this book these are DSM-5 (2013) and ICD-11 (WHO, 2022).

In exploring the psychopathology of trauma, as noted in the introduction to this chapter, we have also drawn from the *Psychodynamic Diagnostic Manual* (PDM-2) which is formulated on the basis that it articulates a psychodynamically oriented diagnosis which bridges the gap between clinical complexity and the need for empirical and methodological validity (Lingiardi & MacWilliams, 2017). It is noted that the PDM explicitly is a taxonomy of people rather than of diseases, and that this description is an effort to describe what one is rather than the symptoms that one has (Lingiardi & MacWilliams, 2017).

Psychodynamic diagnostic classification of complex trauma

Here we quote the definition of complex PTSD as noted in the *Psychodynamic Diagnostic Manual* (Lingiardi & MacWilliams, 2017).

> In CPTSD, untoward events that interfere with optimal personal development between birth and adulthood produce adults who are not intact, who are in some way wounded or vulnerable to subsequent stress. Consequently, another name proposed for this disorder is 'developmental trauma disorder'. Developmental trauma compromises an individual's identity, self-worth and personality, emotional regulation and self-regulation, and ability to relate to others and engage in intimacy. In many, it leads to ongoing despair, lack of meaning and a crisis of spirituality. While PTSD is an atypical response in traumatised adults, developmental trauma may be a very common (and thus the typical) response in traumatised children. Such trauma often goes unrecognised, is misunderstood or denied, or is misdiagnosed by many who assess and treat children. CPTSD is generally associated with a history of chronic neglect, trauma and abuse over the course of childhood [S41.3 pg. 90]

In writing this book we reviewed the cases of Farrokh, Little V and Willow; while they all had official diagnoses of CPTSD in line with the different diagnostic manuals, our aim in this chapter is to offer another perspective rather than repeat a process of aligning their symptomatology taxonomy, DSM-V or ICD-11 taxonomies. Our offer of different perspectives will now be presented in the sections that follow. It is also worth noting that our assumptions and critique of diagnostic systems draws from our joint experiences over decades of supporting people presenting with trauma. Through this we have learnt that recovery from trauma and complex trauma requires restoration of personal control and power for the client. This could be, for example, through restorative trustworthy, healing relationships, which create safety, allow for remembrance and mourning, and promote reconnection with everyday life (Charura & Smith, 2023; Herman, 1992/2022; Sanders & Tolan, 2023).

Conceptualisation of trauma presentation from the lens of our cases

We will now consider from our three cases some conceptualisations of psychopathology from different therapeutic and theoretical orientations.

Case 1: How might we understand Little V's presentations of dissociation and self-injury?

We could, for example, formulate that Little V's avoidance of intimacy in adulthood or the dissociation or somatosensory flooding she experiences when being intimate with a loving partner, was rooted in how she had for many years to disconnect from the physical and emotional pain of being sexually abused as a child. Consequently, in adulthood when facing a context which required her to be vulnerable albeit in a loving relationship, her associative memories emerged, and she became overwhelmed. Thus, the concept of 'the body remembering' (Rothschild, 2000) or as in 'the body keeps the score' (van der Kolk, 2014). Additionally, we could understand her dissociation and self-injury she inflicted from a medical model perspective as her psychopathology, but we could also see it as a creative adjustment to survive the trauma at the time. Furthermore, the self-injury she inflicted on herself, by cutting her thighs with razors, could be understood as a mechanism she developed as another line of defence to feel in touch with her own body in the face of experiences where she had to numb. These presentations of dissociation, somatosensory flooding or self-injury could be understood as the ways in which her psyche had adjusted to defend the pain of the trauma, and her emotional and physical pain when being sexually abused.

Reflection point 6.1

In what other ways might you formulate and understand Little V's symptoms and behaviours in relation to her experiences of trauma?

Case 2: How might we understand Farrokh's presentations of flashbacks, nightmares and functional neurological symptoms?

In considering the case of Farrokh, having arrived in the UK as an asylum seeker, following the multiple traumas he experienced, the torture he had witnessed and experienced, his presentations included flashbacks and nightmares. His symptoms also included repetitive and distressing images and sensations of torture, body pain and aching, and non-epileptic attack seizures. Here we could draw on the power threat meaning framework (PTMF) (Johnstone & Boyle, 2018) to further conceptualise Farrokh's presentation.

The power threat meaning framework is an alternative conceptual approach to the traditional diagnostic model of mental health, and in this case trauma. As an approach it is innovative because it was co-produced by professionals and service users and published by the British Psychological Society (Johnstone et al., 2018). It draws upon a wide range of perspectives, including trauma-informed care (TIC), and offers an evidence-based meta-framework that can be used to support trauma-informed understanding of mental health difficulties (Nikopaschos et al., 2023).

Through supporting Farrokh through therapy from this framework, he developed an identity which is much more imbued with a sense of understanding his trauma journey and the impact of the torture as well as the asylum system on him. His descriptions of being extremely anxious and feeling depressed could be understood as a creative adjustment to managing and coping with extremely distressing circumstances in which power was taken away from him. Through the symptoms he presented, he began to understand that this was a way of his psyche demonstrating the depletion in resources for safety and self-regulation. Thus, he would present as tired, and his body 'would shut off' through having non-epileptic seizures and experiencing other functional neurological symptoms. He often stated that he had no energy and that he was in pain. Through therapy he was able to redefine, reconstruct and reorganise the traumatic experiences about his identity, and shift from the question of 'Why did my own people torture me?' to valuing his inner strength and draw on his faith beliefs that there was a purpose for his survival and being here in the present moment.

Reflection point 6.2

In what other ways might you formulate and understand Farrokh's symptoms and behaviours in relations to his experiences of trauma?

Case 3: How might we understand Willow's presentations of flashbacks, nightmares and functional neurological symptoms?

In considering the case of Willow and the trauma that she has experienced in her lifetime, we concurred that it can be conceptualised in different ways. We know that when Willow was a baby, her parents' relationship was abusive, so it is likely that the home environment may have been unsettling for Willow even if she doesn't remember this period of her life. Within this difficult environment, her parents may have been unable to provide Willow with the nurturing and attunement required to form a secure attachment. If a parent is unable to teach their child how to manage their own emotional needs, the child may develop a weaker sense of self and find it more difficult to relate to others. Willow did, however, form a strong bond with her maternal grandmother, whom she saw regularly. The sudden death of her grandmother, when Willow was 10 years old, was a significant loss for her. Thus, she experienced grief and the absence of emotional security would have led to her feeling extremely anxious in the absence of the familiar environment of her grandmother's house and later her primary school. In addition, as Willow had a diagnosis of autism spectrum disorder (ASD), this provided for us a further point of reflection about her experiences of trauma, neurodiversity and struggles in managing emotions she may experience as difficult to process. Furthermore, the restriction of her eating to the extent that she lost a lot of weight and her periods stopped could be conceptualised as Willow trying to gain some control over her life in response to a sense of lack of autonomy. When formulating Willow's difficulties, in Chapter 4 we suggested that these are understandable responses to an autistic child trying to cope with a complex and traumatic life situation.

Reflection point 6.3

In what other ways might you formulate and understand Willow's symptoms and behaviours in relations to her experiences of trauma?

Thus, for all the clients presented as part of our case studies, we can reframe their diverse presentations of trauma through the lens as 'What happened to you?' rather than 'What's wrong with you?' thereby introducing an alternative to psychiatric diagnosis. This illuminates further the power threat meaning framework (Johnstone & Boyle, 2018) and the emphasis on formulation rather than diagnosis. Here we summarise the six core areas of questioning, which are designed to support narrative construction, from this framework perspective as follows:

1 What has happened to you? (How is power operating in your life?)
2 How did it affect you? (What kind of threats does this pose?)

3 What sense did you make of it? (What is the meaning of these situations and experiences to you?)
4 What did you have to do to survive? (What kind of threat response/s are you using?)
5 What are your strengths? (What access to power resources do you have?)
6 What is your story? (How does this fit together?)

(Johnstone & Boyle, 2018)

A critique we give therefore here is of psychopathology, in describing the experiences that Little V, Farrokh, Willow and many other individuals who experience trauma present with. While from a medical model their presentations could result in diagnosis with PTSD, or CPTSD dissociation, flashbacks, anxiety, depression and so on, the PTMF offers an alternative way to conceptualise trauma experiences as understandable responses to traumatic experiences.

Difficult process (fragile process) and dissociate process

All three clients' symptoms and psychopathology could also be viewed through the lens of Margaret Warner's conceptualisations of '*Difficult processes*' which she also termed as *fragile process*. She suggested that it is a process in which individuals have difficulty in holding their own experience in attention and hence they may feel threatened or misunderstood. Furthermore, Warner defined fragile process as 'a style of process in which clients have difficulty modulating the intensity of core experiences, beginning or ending emotional reactions when socially expected, or taking the points of view of other people without breaking contact with their own experience' (Warner, 2000, p. 115).

Thus, from this perspective, fragile processing has to do with an individual's ability to understand and make sense of incredibly intense, difficult or volatile experiences which are unbearable or impossible to integrate with their experiencing of self (Hauser, 2022). In relation to Little V, Farokh and Willow this framework offered us all as therapists another way to conceptualise their experiences. Furthermore, we viewed their presentations of dissociation as a way to cope with overwhelming experiences – which were completely disconnected or unavailable from their experiencing of the self, owing to the experiences being intense or too painful to be integrated with the self. In line with this, Warner (2000) argued that if the original experience of trauma is extreme, this may also require the client to engage in a further dissociative form of processing that may be exhibited alongside fragile process:

'*Dissociate Process*' is a style of process in which aspects of their person's experience are separated into 'parts' – personified clusters of experience which may be partially or totally unaware of each other's presence. These parts have trance-like qualities, allowing the person to alter perceptions, to alter physiological states, and to hold contradictory beliefs without discomfort. (Warner, 2000, p. 115)

In addition to Warner's perspectives of dissociate process, we are also drawn to the humanistic psychologist Carl Rogers' perspectives on how he approached each person he worked with. Rogers (1961) commented as follows after explaining an incident in which he had been working with difficulty in trying to convince a mother about the root causes of her son's problems and consequently ended up offering that woman successful therapy on her own:

> This incident was one of a number which helped me to experience the fact – only fully realized later–that it is the client who knows what hurts, what direction to go, what problems are crucial, what experiences have been deeply buried. It began to occur to me that unless I had a need to demonstrate my own cleverness and learning I would do better to rely upon the client for the direction of movement in the process. (Rogers, 1961, p. 11–12)

From this we assert that in working with trauma, it is important that the therapist offers this way of being and is engaged in a therapeutic relationship with the client in a way that is collaborative and is open to learning more about the client's process rather than using a diagnostic tool as a 'one size fits all' approach. We discussed in the writing of this book how each client's experiencing of trauma is unique, and even where siblings or family members experienced similar traumas (i.e. childhood abuse, or a car accident) responses often are different. Thus, we advocate for the therapist's openness to learn from each client and to engage in supervision which focuses on exploring different ways of conceptualising client experiences and ways of holding power *with* clients, rather than over clients.

Understanding some trauma presentations and psychopathology through the lens of moral injury

Moral injury, as noted in Chapter 2, resonates with many practitioners who work with trauma and complex trauma because it captures the emotional and spiritual pain that can occur when one's deeply held values are violated (Manguen & Norman, 2021). There are different definitions of moral injury which draw on the description that moral injury relates to including: perpetrating, failing to prevent, bearing witness to or learning about acts that transgress deeply held moral values, beliefs or expectations about rules or codes of conduct (Litz et al., 2009). Furthermore, it has been suggested that for moral injury to occur, individuals must experience a potentially morally injurious event (PMIE) that is perceived as a transgression of deeply held morals, values or individuals engaged in doing something that goes against their values; for example, killing another person/people, acts of omission that are failing to do something in line with values or witnessing or learning about acts that are immoral. Thus, it has been suggested that *moral injury* is the resulting psychological, behavioural, social and sometimes spiritual distress and associated feelings that arise in the individual and these can include, for example, guilt, shame, anger, deep sadness, regret, disgust, self-blame and difficulties with self-forgiveness (Litz et al., 2009; Manguen & Norman, 2021). As a result of this, many people who experience this engage in self-sabotaging behaviours, and we have noted in our clinical practice that individuals presenting with moral injury (for example, military veterans, some refugees or asylum seekers – such as Farrokh presented in our case study) who had been involved as informants in combat situations or had witnessed or been involved in torturing others, often have increased suicidal ideation and elevated risk of suicide attempts. We therefore highlight here that it is important to hold in mind that some trauma presentations and psychopathology with some clients (i.e. in our work with military veterans) can be formulated through the lens of moral injury.

People and not pathology

We have so far presented alternative frameworks and lenses to diagnostic taxonomies [DSM-5, ICD-11] (i.e., the power threat meaning framework, fragile process and moral injury). We now offer another perspective which we apply to the reconceptualisation of psychopathology in trauma work, and for that we draw on the work from person-centred traditions. In line with this we draw on the work of Hipólito et al. (2014) who offered an in-depth examination of psychopathology from a relational person-centred perspective which can aid formulating trauma presentations in light of diagnostic systems (Hipólito et al., 2014). A continual challenge has been what therapists do when faced with two paradigms within the therapeutic relationship, one being the psychiatric diagnostic biomedical model and the other being the psychotherapeutic holistic non-medical model.

Hipólito et al. (2014) argued that psychological therapy practitioners must have knowledge and skills to be able to use the most suitable 'diagnostic' approach depending on the specific clinical situations, in order to make decisions in terms of treatment, including cases of involuntary commitment. Furthermore, they also argued that working with clients who may be referred for psychological therapeutic support therefore requires therapists to have the ability to be aware of the impact the psychiatric system may have on clients. Thus, they proposed that within such therapeutic relationships, a paradigm shift is necessary for all modalities, from a position of focusing on diagnosis, labelling and treating to a position of co-development of a therapeutic relationship that is, in itself, a facilitator of change and can help reduce the distress that the clients may be experiencing (Hipólito et al., 2014).

The suggestion is that psychopathology can be understood through the combination of traumas that took place throughout the person's life, both about the individual's strengths and with regard to acting upon those strengths, in order for change and growth to ensue (Hipólito et al., 2014).

Another perspective we align with is that of Sanders and Tolan (2023) whose edited book, *People Not Pathology: Freeing therapy from the medical model*

(Sanders & Tolan, 2023) offered an exposition of a diversity of perspectives which evaluate and critique the concept of psychopathology. They proposed a demedicalised approach, thereby offering challenges to the medicalisation of psychological distress and enduring disturbing experiences. This frees therapy from the medical models so offering therapists alternative models to diagnosis while enabling them to work with clients who may present with difficulties (Sanders & Tolan, 2023).

Conclusion

Here we consider the necessity of a relational trauma-informed approach to psychopathology and argue that the essence of a traumatic experience is a sense of the lack of a primary condition – that of connection. In traumatic experience, the individual feels entirely alone. In the context of working through the trauma in psychotherapy with people in their darkest moments, a relational approach at heart is about the therapist stepping into the loneliness, into that solitary space, and being there (Charura & Smith, 2024; Smith & Charura, 2024). This could almost be seen as the beginning of mapping what the individual deeply requires, that is, the capacity to re-enter into relationship in the future without the threat of the alienation and trauma being triggered in the here and now. Trauma psychoeducation is important, particularly in helping the client to realise that engaging with the nature of memory is a fluid, changing structure. As part of psychoeducation it is important for clients to be aware that if they engage with a trauma memory, the psychosomato-sensory experience and feelings which may have been experienced at the time of the trauma, can become triggered in the present moment. Alongside this, being grounded and feeling safe is central to a relational approach to working with trauma. Therefore, what we are proposing is that trauma that happens can also occur in relationship with the working through of the trauma. Charura and Smith argued (2023, p.302) that 'a relational approach posits that trauma happens in and through relationships and it can therefore also be argued that processing trauma, change, and growth can occur through the co-creation of the therapeutic relationship'. We assert that when working with psychopathology, from a trauma perspective, in the therapeutic relationship what the therapist engages with is the client's/patients' deep sense of alienation, aloneness and the solitariness that the client/patient experiences. In those moments the therapist does their utmost to understand the other; they aim to be present to the detail, the fear, the angst or whatever it is that's emerging with the clients. This means that if we consider that each human being has within themselves the internal resources to grow, to become more complex as a being through their capacity for self-organisation, then with the right therapeutic support, the individual can move towards their potential for self-healing and for self-fulfilment (which Rogers 1959 postulated as hyper-complexity) within their own frame of reference; from this perspective, there is no longer a place for a label that smothers their capacity for growth and healing (Hipólito et al., 2014). This creates an opportunity within the therapeutic relationship for a co-creation of meaning and self-understanding of the client's subjective experience of trauma which goes beyond giving a label and offering 'treatment' (Hipólito et al., 2014).

In this chapter our intention has been to offer perspectives that enable a multiplicity of perspectives and critique of diagnostic models and frameworks, that enable us to understand clients, their lived experiences of trauma and consequent responses rather than a view of 'what one has' type of pathology. We also want to highlight here, as noted by O'Brien and Charura (2022; 2023), that there is an urgent need to better understand manifestations of embodied trauma, with a focus on providing a culturally informed psychological assessment method, formulation, treatment plan and early intervention for those in distress. Thus, we share their critique of psychopathology and the limitations of Eurocentric frameworks that ignore the cultural context and belief systems of many clients who present with trauma. In concluding, we concur with Lingiardi and McWilliams (2017) who argued that without a counterpoint to the current tendency to focus more and more narrowly on discrete disorder categories, the therapeutic relationship may be jeopardised and even damaged. This has been one of our reasons of including a psychopathology chapter which invites the reader to consider a diversity of classification systems and non-diagnostic frameworks to the mental health and trauma presentations. We end this chapter with some reflection points for you to consider and engage with.

Reflection point 6.4

1 What questions and challenges have struck you in reading this chapter?
2 Having covered psychology from DSM, ICD-11, PDM and the power threat meaning framework, what critical approaches help you in your understanding of psychopathology trauma presentations?
3 What are the benefits and critique of diagnostic criteria and engaging with these criteria?

7

Trauma therapy: contemporary approaches and potential limitations

Mark McFetridge, Emma Bradshaw and Divine Charura

Overview

- This chapter will consider the value of NICE guideline recommended therapies.
- It aims to stimulate thought regarding the dominance of NICE Guidelines, and the unintended consequences of mandated therapies.
- We consider possibilities for the future of trauma therapy in the post-Covid-19 era.

Psychological therapies for PTSD

We are fortunate, that together with our clients, we have been able to develop trauma therapies with a good evidence base supporting their effectiveness. It has been formally acknowledged that psychological therapies for PTSD are effective (NICE, 2018) and indeed more effective than interventions from other paradigms. This is a message of hope we can offer our traumatised clients, and a sense of containment we may benefit from ourselves as their therapist or practitioner psychologist.

Within the UK, the first NICE Guideline for PTSD (National Institute for Health and Care Excellence, 2005) identified psychological therapies as more effective than psychotropic medication, and two particular psychological therapies as possessing 'Grade-A' evidence for their effectiveness: trauma-focused cognitive behavioural therapy (tf-CBT), and eye movement desensitisation and reprocessing (EMDR).

The evidence base for these therapies has grown further since this time and has been consolidated in several systematic reviews of the literature (e.g. Lewis et al., 2020) and an updated NICE guideline for PTSD (NICE, 2018). However, while there are many other approaches and trauma therapies in practice (let alone a personalised multimodal therapy derived from a formulation with your client), no further therapies have been added to this recommended list for UK NHS resource implementation.

It may be that other therapies lack the effectiveness of tf-CBT and EMDR, or that they may lack the evidence to demonstrate their effectiveness. This may appear the same thing at first sight, but it is crucially important for us to appreciate they are not. It is ironic that if we had believed that *lack of evidence means evidence of lack* in the past, we would not be in the position we are now to offer these very therapies.

Perhaps we can all develop complacency when things appear to be going well; I (MM) am ashamed to admit that when I was asked by students in 1996 what I thought about a new strange technique (EMDR), my response (albeit unspoken, but certainly felt) was that we didn't need to explore such a 'wacky' therapy as our existing therapies were useful and understandable in terms of theory (unlike EMDR). I partially redeemed myself by training in EMDR that year and later undertaking research (McFetridge, 2001) examining the process and outcomes of EMDR, entailing further training with Francine Shapiro in New York in 1998 (the things we do for research!).

I still expected the protocol-adherent EMDR provided to chronically traumatised people to be found lacking in effectiveness, except it wasn't (far from it, in fact). I learned from this, among other things, that it is dangerously easy to dismiss from a place of comfort; perhaps this is merely the converse of the old proverb *Necessity is the mother of invention*? We should perhaps pay renewed attention to old wisdom.

Therefore, there is a danger we may unwittingly limit our opportunity to establish the future potential effectiveness of a broader range of trauma therapies because we already have therapies that 'work'. These existing therapies may not work as well as future developments, however, particularly for different individuals in different settings and from different cultures.

A further concern raised by Green and Latchford (2012) concerns the bias that may be introduced by the assumptions within the process, for example, that the best possible evidence (rated 'A' by NICE) is from a double-blind randomised controlled trial (RCT). To be fair to NICE, this is explicitly stated within the methodology and therefore far from hidden. However, many of us who consult the NICE guideline may be unaware of these assumptions, for example, some NHS commissioners and operational managers may lack awareness of the implications of this statistical premise.

One implication, of which we may be unaware, is that our client would have probably been excluded from the research trials their mandated NHS therapy is derived from. Most complex clients seen by practitioner psychologists have more than one clearly defined difficulty or symptomatic presentation, often referred to as *comorbidity*. RCTs of a psychological condition such as PTSD generally exclude potential participants from the trial who have comorbid depression, alcohol or substance misuse, dissociation or voice-hearing. This is despite us having known for some time that all these symptoms, or comorbid difficulties, may indeed be secondary to a history of trauma (van der Kolk, 2014). The complex client with whom we work and employ an evidence-based therapy would very likely never have been selected to contribute to the evidence base underlying the form of therapy now recommended for them!

This is not to say, however, that a particular evidence-based therapy will prove unhelpful for them, but we will never know whether a different therapy may have been more effective for them as an individual.

If we pause to think, we may have little difficulty with the idea that different therapies will not be equally effective for all individuals. It has been found in studies of specific client groups (e.g. US military veterans) that those not responding positively following nine sessions are unlikely to go on to experience a good outcome with trauma-focused therapy for PTSD (Sripada et al., 2020). Active monitoring of response to therapy was recommended by the authors as a cue to consider other approaches for our client.

Cultural heritage and therapy

One important aspect of potential difference and individuality is our cultural heritage. Many surnames in the West contain ancient reference to this, whether to profession (e.g., Cooper, Taylor) or paternity (e.g., MacDonald, McLean). People from certain cultures still retain this social sense of identity and introduce themselves with greater reference to their home or group of belonging, than to their individuality. If these variations in sense of identity are sufficiently important to be embedded within the way we define ourselves to others, it is possible that mandated therapies may fail to take account of these cultural differences. We therefore need to be aware of the potential bias that may underlie the evidence base for a given therapy and remain open to considering whether this is necessarily the most effective intervention for our client. I (MM) recall a respected researcher and clinician, who had developed a well-known mode of therapy, presenting a keynote paper at a conference. Following the presentation during questions, a member of the audience stood up and stated, 'I was a participant in this research trial, and this therapy saved my life'. Rather than merely accepting the opportunity to bask in this glowing endorsement, the presenter replied, 'Thank you, but we will never know whether another therapy would have given you even more of a life'. This wise and reflective response reflects a stance from which the next paradigm shift in psychological therapies for trauma is possible, if we were all to adopt it.

Historically, much of what we understand about PTSD was derived from the psychological casualties of war, particularly veterans of the Vietnam war (Herman, 1992/2022). Armed conflict has few certain outcomes; but these include death, destruction and trauma. At the time of writing, we are anticipating the psychological casualties of the protracted and bloody war in the Ukraine (Nalyvaiko, 2023), and from the conflict in Palestine and Israel. Do we think that the formalised therapies derived from our European research are equally sensitive to the cultural needs and social norms of these potentially traumatised individuals?

Following the Balkan civil war (1992–1995) a young Bosnian man was referred to our trauma service by a local refugee charity; he had been brutalised and tortured before he and his young family were able to escape to the UK. I (MM) did not speak Bosnian, he did not speak English, but the solution was hoped by others to be in EMDR (less of a 'talking therapy' and still unusual in late 1996), with an interpreter to assist if necessary. I was aware of the weight of expectation of others wanting to help Bruno by facilitating his referral to our specialist trauma service. However, was this young man traumatised and meeting diagnostic criteria for PTSD? (*Yes*); was it safe to undertake trauma therapy? (*Yes*); was this therapy appropriate to the individual's expressed needs and goals? (Actually, and inconveniently, *No*). I soon came to appreciate that Bruno was a displaced husband and father and a skilled car mechanic who was not yet in the right place, nor the right time, to address his intrusive traumatic memories of the torture he had survived. Bruno's needs were for the safety and stability of his family, to regain some sense of control of his life, of his sense of identity, and importantly his self-esteem and role as the 'provider' for his family. The non-trauma-focused therapeutic intervention deriving from this formulation was to find Bruno opportunity to work as a (volunteer) mechanic in a local garage, alongside other men. This was not easy to facilitate within a state system that would provide healthcare for refugees, but emphatically not offer employment. However, this was the non-verbal therapy this traumatised man really required, until he and his family could return to the safe home where he felt they belonged. I would never know whether Bruno had later chosen to address his traumatic memories with a Bosnian clinician, but I had a deep sense that he had been helped with what was more personally, culturally and temporally appropriate by this British clinician.

Other trauma therapies

Many years ago, Samuel Tuke (1813), wrote that one of our key therapeutic aims is (to) *excite the capabilities of patients*. He was describing the particularly unconventional approach, with its unusually positive outcomes, of the Retreat, York, UK. He retrospectively named this *moral therapy*, but this approach to mental health care had been primarily developed from the principles and values of Quakerism. The Retreat, York is considered the home of occupational therapy as a helping profession within the UK, with its emphasis on the importance of useful occupation, alongside valuing communalism, the healing power of everyday relationships, our physical and social environment, spirituality and non-violence. The work at the Retreat has (perhaps ironically) been considered the foundation of the therapeutic community (TC) group approach developed during the Second World War (1939–1945) to treat the overwhelming numbers of traumatised soldiers returning home. Therapeutic communities, with their relational approach to helping clients (so commonly affected by interpersonal trauma) have more recently reported significant improvements in trauma-related symptoms, and in the sense of self, with these benefits maintaining decades after therapy (McFetridge et al., 2015; McFetridge & Coakes, 2010).

Narrative exposure therapy

It is also within conflict-beset areas of the world that other trauma therapies have been developed, out of need and limited resource. Narrative exposure therapy (NET) was originally developed for treating survivors of war and torture and has been extensively employed in the Democratic Republic of Congo, Burundi and in North Korea. Some of the novel aspects of NET include the survivor's use of string, stones and flowers to depict their lifeline, together with positive and negative life events (Siehl et al., 2021). Individuals are supported to systematically expose themselves to the memories, following which the listener reads a collated account of the life experiences back to the individual. Due to the greater need than limited resources permit in many post-conflict settings, local community members have been trained to facilitate NET within their own communities. This approach has been further developed to address traumatic experience within a collective, communal or tribal culture (Koebach & Robjant, 2021). Termed NETfacts, the process includes a community lifeline exercise, again using flowers and stones for positive and negative events, and additionally the use of sticks to represent active involvement in violence towards others.

Despite these limited resources and frequent delivery by non-professionally trained lay therapists, NET has been found to be effective in processing traumatic memories. A metanalysis of 89 RCTs of psychotherapies for PTSD (Yunitri et al., 2023) concluded that NET, along with CPT and EMDR were the therapies most likely to lead to the loss of a PTSD diagnosis, i.e. symptomatic improvement such that an individual no longer meets criteria. It is therefore both impressive, and challenging of our orthodoxy, that a therapy such as NET can be found to be as equally effective as such established therapies as EMDR.

The therapeutic relationship

Yunitri et al. (2023) also noted a general lack of attention to the therapeutic relationship in most formal trauma therapies and proposed that clinical outcomes might be further improved significantly by simultaneous attention to this.

This comes as little surprise to those of us with experience of stepping into the past alongside our clients; trust, safety and containment are relational factors that intuitively moderate how willing an individual is to allow themselves to be vulnerable in the process of therapy. There is evidence to suggest that this willingness on the part of our clients to risk their experiencing of greater emotional pain can be associated with more therapeutic gain from trauma therapy (McFetridge, 2001). Therefore, the therapeutic relationship may offer the necessary relational conditions, (like a catalyst), for the additional potential therapeutic effect of any given intervention to be realised.

Therapeutic flexibility, in the form of 'modular therapy', has been suggested to be potentially more effective and acceptable to clients with complex PTSD (Karatzias & Cloitre, 2019). Within this approach, therapist and client together determine the choice from among empirically supported interventions, with a process of implementing this, then reviewing progress and gains, and repeating. The order of delivery of intervention is decided by reference to symptoms that are impairing, severe and considered relevant by the client.

EMDR

A limitation of current approaches raised by some authors concerns their genesis, or how they were developed. Some therapeutic approaches have not derived from established psychological theory. EMDR is one of the examples of the serendipity of the development of a therapeutic approach; in this case beginning with the 'walk in the park' taken by Francine Shapiro (Shapiro, 2018). She noticed the distress she experienced (associated with a health issue), lessened following her lunchtime walk, and so set about with colleagues researching what may have caused this reduction. This led to the identification of eye movements (or 'alternating rhythmic stimuli') as the potential active ingredient, with further development leading to the addition of cognitive, affective and somatic elements of the therapeutic approach. Initially the eye movements were thought to be like those of dream (REM – rapid eye movement) sleep and hypothesised to provide a similar beneficial processing function. Now EMDR is a mainstream therapy for PTSD it is difficult to appreciate just how much of a paradigm shift it represented. Evidence from RCTs continued to amass (largely due to Shapiro herself, initially) and yet we still didn't understand how the therapy was working, beyond a plausible rationale.

Cognitive therapy

The most well-known and widely utilised clinical approach to treating PTSD within UK statutory mental health services is based on the cognitive model of Anke Ehlers and David Clark (Ehlers & Clark, 2000). This form of cognitive therapy is unusual (and distinct from EMDR) in that the intervention is derived directly from a theoretical model of understanding of PTSD. This approach has been further developed by Emily Holmes and colleagues, with the explicit aim of identifying simple interventions derived from an understanding of traumatic memory, that can have the greatest population impact (Kanstrup et al., 2021). An early study demonstrated that asking potentially traumatised individuals presenting to Accident & Emergency departments to undertake a visuospatial task (a Tetris puzzle) resulted in lower rates of PTSD symptoms than those in a control group. This intervention was derived from a theoretical understanding of traumatic memory; that giving a visuospatial 'load' would impair the ability to consolidate sensory memories of the potentially traumatic event. This would then lead to a reduction in flashbacks and other forms of re-experiencing. This line of research is appealing in both its theory–practice links, and in its striving for the greatest possible population impact within our limited mental health resources.

The post-Covid-19 era

One of the psychological changes in our communities reported by many in this post-Covid-19 era is a greater appreciation of the connection and real contact with others. It is almost dystopian now to recall that in the UK we were told, and legally bound, by our Prime Minister to stay at home and to avoid contact with anyone outside our household. Other people could unwittingly kill you with their transmission of the virus and, perhaps worse, you might in turn infect your family. We were thankful for videoconferencing as a proxy for human contact, but it soon lost its social promise for many of us. Personally, I (MM) worried that the seductive convenience and ease of virtual meetings might signal the death of the actual face-to-face meeting together of colleagues, or of clinician and client. There were reports however of some neurodivergent clients, who found social interaction difficult, adapting very well to this shift: a unique adaption of the total social environment to suit some individuals' communication style and preference. For those of us who did not share this preference, perhaps our own psychological distress of this time may serve as an important lesson of the effect of having normative rules of relating that are ego dystonic. We should strive to remember those feelings and learning in order to help our appreciation of the experience of some neurodivergent clients.

Since Covid-19, the range of our forms of interaction has been extended; what was thought impossible is now routine (i.e. remote meetings and clinical consultations) and there is a newfound gratitude for the human encounter with its unique embedded eye contact. Actual eye contact may well be a powerful form of communication and emotional co-regulation within itself, as many a parent of a new-born will know, and one that is absent from the remote meeting. Some have suggested that our additional post-Covid appreciation of nature and our green spaces might be combined with the real encounter in the form of 'walking meetings' (Bornioli, 2023). Perhaps this novel approach might be explored further and evaluated for the potential of dual processing and the conducive setting offered, to some, for their therapeutic work.

More recently, novel PTSD interventions have also been developed that derive from an understanding of the neuropsychological functioning thought to underpin our client's traumatic memory. A study of the potential effectiveness of neurofeedback-assisted downregulation of the amygdala (a brain structure within the limbic system associated with our experiencing of emotion) found that participants were indeed able to achieve this reduced activation, compared to a control group. However, no significant differences were found between the groups in the effect of this on PTSD symptoms (Zhao et al., 2023). The authors suggest the notable reduction in PTSD symptoms in the control group contributed to this lack of group difference. We should be curious about why the control group improved in symptomatology however, despite 'sham' training that did not help participants to better regulate their amygdala. There are, after all, examples of control group interventions later being adopted as effective therapies after similarly demonstrating unexpected benefits within an RCT, e.g. structured clinical management (Vogt & Norman, 2019). Given that PTSD can strip away an individual's sense of control, it may be that the biofeedback (even sham) may still be therapeutic by providing this sense of control? Perhaps this is the active ingredient that then acts to down-regulate the amygdala. This remains to be further explored and the hypothesised mechanism to be tested (perhaps by someone seeking a doctoral research project?).

Visuospatial tasks that prompt our clients to consider a broader perspective of the trauma scene and events have been found to be successful in reducing reported traumatic symptoms and improvements in wellbeing (Miller, 2022). This and other novel approaches are yet to be rigorously evaluated; however, as we have noted, lack of evidence is not the same as evidence of lack, and we should continue to be open to new developments and potential therapeutic advancements in our field.

Conclusion

In conclusion, it is of central importance that we can continue to broaden the range of effective therapeutic interventions we are able to offer to meet the diverse needs of our future clients. There is a danger that the progress that has permitted development of our existing effective therapies for PTSD may stall, due to the unintended consequences of our systems of good practice. To continue with our progress will require an open stance of us all, and a collective culture of enquiry. In this way we will benefit from further paradigm shifts and improvements in psychological therapy for PTSD and perhaps discover the 'next' EMDR.

Reflection point 7.1

1 What do you think are the potential benefits and limitations of an evidence-based therapy approach?
2 What are you curious about within the field of trauma and trauma therapy?
3 What do you think are the potential obstacles to you developing a further understanding of trauma, and how might you address these?

8 Critical perspectives: reflecting on our understanding of trauma and recovery

Mark McFetridge, Divine Charura and Emma Bradshaw

Overview

- This chapter offers a critique of our current understanding of traumatic memory and its potential manifestations.
- We consider the accuracy of flashbacks and the account of Charles Dickens, after the Staplehurst railway crash of 1865.
- We explore 'moral injury', highlighted by the experiences of key workers during the peak of the Covid-19 pandemic.
- We suggest caution in what we presume in our work with people who have experienced potentially traumatic events.

Before addressing some surprising issues we have encountered in our work with traumatised people, we invite you to consider this question in Reflection point 8.1:

Reflection point 8.1

Are flashbacks and other forms of re-experiencing trauma, by their nature, accurate memories?

Flashbacks and Charles Dickens

We are all aware of the fallibility of everyday memory; we forget and misremember on a regular basis. However, many of us presume that the re-experiencing of trauma, given its predominantly non-verbal form, is an accurate and reliable memory of what happened. There is an old saying, long preceding digital photoshop and artificial intelligence (AI), that '*the camera never lies*'. In a similar way, many of us have thought that such a primary, or sensory, form of memory precedes our interpretation and therefore the potential for introducing error. If, in twentieth century Western popular film or literature, the main character unfortunately suffered an amnesia for crucial aspects of their experience then hypnosis was considered a means of accessing these primary representations of events, or memories. This carries an assumption that these sensory or verbally inaccessible memories are accurate, once revealed.

In 1865, the celebrated author Charles Dickens was travelling through Kent in a railway carriage together with a female friend and her chaperoning aunt. The train suddenly derailed as it passed over a viaduct in Staplehurst, upending some carriages with their passengers and sending others crashing below. We know many of the details of this event from letters to his close friend, John Forster. Dickens described, in one letter to his friend, how he had climbed out of the carriage window to assist for several hours among the dead and dying, before leaving the horrific scene (Forster, 1876).

We had yet to clearly identify post-traumatic stress disorder in 1865. At this time forms of mental affliction were commonly named according to either their apparent precipitating events, e.g. 'railway shaking' (following the frequent early rail incidents) or by a predominant somatic symptom e.g. 'irritable heart' (experienced by Florence Nightingale's patients of the Crimean war 1853–56).

Dickens wrote in detail about how the railway accident had severely affected him, including how he would later experience a clear and compelling sense of falling to one side if his horse-drawn carriage was '*to approach anything like speed*'. This, he added, was accompanied by a level of distress he found extremely difficult to express. The fact that one of our most celebrated authors struggled to put his distress into words may be a helpful reassurance to our clients who are frustrated and self-critical of their own difficulty with this. Dickens clearly attributed these phenomena to his previous experience of the Staplehurst rail crash, and the effects of railway shaking. When reading his account of a serious accident involving significant loss of life and of his involvement in the aftermath, we may wonder if Dickens was experiencing symptoms associated with post-traumatic stress disorder?

A phenomenon that Dickens noted with admirable curiosity, however, was that his somatosensory re-experiencing of the derailing carriage was not entirely accurate. He experienced flashbacks or *body-memories* contralateral to the original event. It was widely known and recorded that the Staplehurst train had derailed in the direction opposite to Dicken's somatosensory re-experiencing of falling to one side.

This account of Dickens, and the conundrum it represents, remained on the library shelf for many decades. Unfortunately, as busy clinicians we tend not to look to other shelves or subject areas outside our field. However, when one day a client was describing her experience of a traumatic motor vehicle accident, something about it felt reminiscent of Dicken's experience (the *Ghost of Christmas past?*, Dickens 1868). During the fourth clinical session together, client and practitioner psychologist were actively engaging with exposure to the client's memory of her traumatic car crash. The client accompanied her first-person narration of the immediate aftermath with a behavioural enaction: 'The steering wheel airbag has exploded. I can see smoke; the car is on fire (*see endnote). I am trying to unfasten my seatbelt' (she enacts unfastening of the seatbelt with her left hand from the right of her seat). The client continues her account, and then I (MM) ask her to repeat from the beginning, prompting her for further detail. Again, the client reaches across her body and unfastens her seatbelt from the right with her left hand.

Towards the end of the session, I attempt to consolidate and contextualise the information gained from the session with her. The client is asked if she was driving a conventional right-hand drive car (the accident occurred in the UK). The client reports that she was, and it had a seatbelt that came from the driver's right shoulder and fixed to the left of her waist. When the discrepancy between her seatbelt location and her behavioural enaction of unfastening is sensitively pointed out, the client expresses confusion and an inability to reconcile this. She continues to believe, from her visual and proprioceptive recall, that she had unfastened a seatbelt from her right side.

How might these reported discrepancies between reported traumatic memories and physical reality be understood? Could these perhaps have been the manifestations of an out-of-body experience? After all, peri-traumatic dissociation has long been known to potentially accompany the experience of extreme emotional arousal, or feeling out of control (Lensvelt-Mulders et al., 2008; van der Hart et al., 2008). Perhaps both Dickens and our client were re-enacting a somatic memory from a safer and detached perspective, as if looking down on the overwhelming scene?

These conundrums, together with other clinical reports of unusual traumatic memory, deserve further examination, research and interdisciplinary collaboration. If we pay attention to what we struggle to explain within our current models, sit with this uncertainty and reflect on it with colleagues, we will continue to enhance our understanding.

When we consider the validity of the diagnostic criteria for PTSD (as detailed in Chapter 6), it is worth bearing in mind that the two current diagnostic manuals do not entirely agree with one another. The main difference between the two sets of diagnostic criteria for PTSD is that there are three specific core symptom areas in ICD-11 (2022), while DSM-5TR (2023) still retains a broader requirement for a fourth. This is partly due to the inclusion of the additional diagnosis of complex PTSD within ICD-11, whereas DSM-5TR attempts to address this within the diagnosis of PTSD alone by the further inclusion of more generalised symptoms. One consequence of this, therefore, is that it is possible for our client (perhaps also Dickens retrospectively?) to meet criteria for PTSD within DSM-5TR, but not within ICD-11. This is a useful reminder that diagnostic manuals and models should not be taken as *the Truth*, but rather merely as one version of this, at one point in time.

Moral injury

Before most of us had heard of pandemics, (and certainly of Covid-19) there were reports of a form of psychological injury that did not entirely fit with the diagnostic criteria or the common conceptualisation of PTSD. This had been termed 'moral injury' previously (as noted in Chapter 6) and had mainly appeared in research involving military combat veterans (Frankfurt & Frazier, 2016). Moral injury has been defined as 'the lasting emotional, cognitive, behavioural, social, and/or spiritual impact of exposure to a potentially morally injurious event, such as perpetrating, failing to prevent, bearing witness to, or learning about acts that transgress deeply held moral beliefs or expectations' (Litz et al., 2009, p.700). People may struggle with guilt, self-disgust or a lack of self-compassion with related self-sabotaging or self-punishing behaviours (Jinkerson, 2016).

When healthcare staff became overwhelmed by the numbers of desperately ill and dying patients with Covid-19, moral injury was thought to have become more widespread. It certainly became more mainstream within the evaluation and research undertaken during this time (Greene et al., 2023). Decisions about who was to live or to die were frequently having to be made by healthcare staff, without sufficient time or attention given to the potentially psychologically damaging effects of this personal responsibility. Furthermore, healthcare staff also became more isolated from the outside world, perhaps exacerbated by the strategy of casting the NHS as the archetypal 'hero' in the fight against the 'villain' virus. It is hard to complain, or protest, as a hero, but many healthcare staff would rather have been clapped-for less and protected more. This public perception of heroic healthcare staff did not match the self-perceptions of many staff members, with health and social care staff developing a growing sense of feeling let down or abandoned by their managers, leaders and the wider system.

Shay (2014) had previously suggested that the personal experience of betrayal by an authority, or other in a position of power in relation to the individual, may also be a cause of a moral injury. This indeed appeared to be possible from the studies of self-reports of health and social care staff of the Covid-19 period. Greene et al. (2023) asked over a thousand frontline healthcare workers deployed during the Covid-19 pandemic about their experiences and symptoms. They found betrayal-related, potentially morally injurious events were a significant predictor of probable PTSD or of probable CPTSD. This is referred to as a 'probable' diagnosis as it was not possible within the research, given the circumstances, to include a definitive diagnostic interview. Greene et al. (2023), however, reported a probable rate of ICD-11 PTSD of 8.3 per cent, and 14.2 per cent for probable CPTSD. Not having personal protective equipment (PPE) available to the healthcare worker on a reliable basis was the only factor that reliably predicted a staff member meeting probable diagnosis for CPTSD, rather than for PTSD. The failure, as a frontline healthcare worker, to be provided with the PPE known to be required to maintain your safety at work could understandably lead to the experience (i.e. the affect, cognitive and behavioural response) of having been 'let down' or betrayed by the parental organisation. This is likely to have been exacerbated under the extreme duress of the time, with exhausting working hours, insufficient respite and repeating human tragedy.

At the time of writing, some three years after the worst of the Covid-19 experience, a large group of former NHS staff are attempting to bring a legal case against their employer for failure to adequately prevent them from contracting the virus at work and subsequently developing 'long-Covid' and subsequent loss of their careers.

There are also regular UK media reports of desperately low morale within the NHS, high sickness and absenteeism, as well as impossibly long waiting lists for treatment.

Could this, at least in part, be the psychological and service related 'fall-out' for the morally injurious experiences of the healthcare workers within the NHS? It would not be the first time this has happened: there was extreme difficulty in recruiting mental health nurses in the years following the end of the Second World War (1945). Improvements in pay and conditions were introduced, but unfortunately this had little benefit on the recruitment difficulty; 'taking the country as a whole, the nursing profession is passing through a real crisis' (Pool, 1946). Perhaps in exasperation, Dr Pool went on to report (in) 'my own view...it is not a wages problem at all but one aspect of the spiritual decadence of our time'. We have considered the relational effect of a felt sense of betrayal by leaders and organisations, but Pool (1946) raises (albeit with a tinge of criticism) the question of the effect of critical events on our spirituality.

Spirituality

Certainly, spirituality receives very little attention in general within psychiatric diagnostic criteria, and within PTSD in particular. But what do we mean here by spirituality? Well, we do not necessarily mean *religion*. An individual's sense of spirituality *may* be derived from their formal religion and related practices, but for many people their spirituality is entirely unrelated to religion and is derived from elsewhere. The Royal College of Psychiatrists have an established Spirituality special interest group, and in 2006 it offered the following definition:

> (spirituality is) *identified with experiencing a deep-seated sense of meaning and purpose in life, together with a sense of belonging. It is about acceptance, integration and wholeness.* (Salem, 2006, p.2)

A further attempt to capture the essence of spirituality was developed by a spirituality interest group comprising the staff and clients of the Retreat, York. It offered a concise definition of spirituality as:

> *What uplifts us, what makes us whole, what connects us.* (The Retreat York, S Group, 2011)

Kao et al. (2020) reviewed the evidence for a potential relationship between our sense of spirituality and our mental health. They suggested the social aspects of religious involvement can have a buffering effect against depression and, to a lesser extent, for mental health in general. This cannot be presumed to be a specific effect of spirituality per se, however. A further study examined the brains and neuroanatomical correlates of depression, finding evidence suggestive of the positive effect of spirituality on brain structure. Individuals at high risk of depression were found to have a greater thinning of the cerebral cortex. However, this cortical thinning was significantly less for those who reported religion or spirituality as very important to them (Miller et al., 2014). The authors suggest that it is therefore possible that engagement with spirituality or religion may buffer us from the harmful effects of depression.

What of the relationship between spirituality, or religion, and the consequence of trauma? Formal religion is of central importance to many people and can be a source of great resilience and solace. In some cases, however, the interpretation of religious beliefs could add to the burden of those individuals who have experienced interpersonal trauma, especially those considered shameful, e.g. rape. For the traumatised individual there may also be implications, via their meaning-making, for their relationship with their God or higher being (e.g. how could a benign God let this happen?). This could equally be the case for an individual whose sense of spirituality is derived from nature (e.g. nature is cruel) or from human relationships (e.g. people on social media are cruel). If the traumatic event we endured diminishes our opportunity to continue to engage in a spiritual practice previously important to us, it can be reasonably assumed there will be additional mental health consequences for us.

Our spiritual disconnect can also derive from our thoughts and meaning making during the traumatic event (i.e. peri-traumatic). These cognitions, preserved in time and unchallenged, may then continue to influence our memory, thinking and responses. The inspirational poem *Footsteps in the sand* (Stevenson, 1939) describes two sets of footprints, which then become one. In the poem, the individual exclaims to their God, 'I have noticed that during the most trying periods of my life there have only been one set of footprints in the sand. Why when I needed you most, have you not been there for me?' In the poem, God replies, 'the times when you have seen only one set of footprints is when I carried you'. This poem resonates with our experience of clients who have come to make, facilitated by the therapeutic process, significant shifts in understanding of the context to their traumatic experiences. Some have realised that while they felt deeply alone at the time, they were not alone; some have 'realised' that they did not in fact die; some have realised that despite the shame they have felt, people do in fact accept and believe them.

Trauma and history

Judith Herman (1992/2022) in her key text *Trauma and Recovery*, questioned why we need to repeatedly relearn what we already know. Herman noted, by the end of the First World War (1914–1918) our understanding of 'shell shock' had been advanced by the treatment of the traumatised war poet Captain

Siegfried Sassoon, by the psychologist W.H.R. Rivers. In the early days of the war, those traumatised by the relentless death and horror they endured were considered cowards and executed by firing squad. More fortunate individuals were deemed to require the new technology of electric shock treatment, termed *Faradization*, initially applied to the paralysed limbs and then to more sensitive parts of the body. Sassoon, however, was fortunate to be offered the opportunity to meet and talk with Rivers each day and was encouraged to resume his emotional expression and creativity through the writing of poetry. Sassoon went on to recover and he returned to the front line to lead his men again, fortunately surviving the war. Rivers later wrote about his experience of successfully treating the traumatic neuroses following the war (Rivers, 1918). Unfortunately, as Herman (1992/2022) sadly notes, by the Second World War (1939–1945) our understanding of recognising and treating the potentially traumatising effect of warfare had for some reason, to be developed once again.

Perhaps, after potentially traumatic events affecting whole communities, there can be a tension between 'never forgetting' and 'moving on'. Survivors of these mass events may want their children to have a future that is very different from their own past, and yet also want them to remember that people can do unthinkable things to others and therefore prevent this from recurring. Perhaps it is because these events are so extreme as to be 'unthinkable' with 'unspeakable acts', that they may become preconscious and non-verbal in the intergenerational transmission of this traumatic experience. There is a deeply moving, yet hopeful, account of the intergenerational traumatic effects of the colonisation of indigenous aboriginal people (Australian Foundation for Indigenous sustainable health, 2019). It highlights the unintended negative effect of parents sharing their traumatic stories with their children. The problem, however, is that their children no longer have the traditional ways of buffering the impact of these stories since the cultural changes that accompanied colonisation. The result is described as a generation of 'broken youth' with severe mental health problems and substance abuse. The message of hope conveyed by the Australian Foundation emphasises the importance of indigenous people regaining a cultural connection with each other, with the land and with nature, to become once again resilient to life's challenges.

This may also be helpful in highlighting a potential blind spot for the Western practitioner psychologist and for our prevailing theories. From within an individualistic society, we tend to make sense of, and 'treat' people as individuals rather than formulating and intervening with groups, systems and society. We will further consider how we might adopt a more systemic perspective within Chapter 10.

The finding that it was an interpersonal event during the Covid-19 pandemic (the failure of those in power to provide personal protective equipment) that proved the factor predicting CPTSD (Greene et al., 2023) reminds us that it has long been thought that interpersonal traumas have much wider ranging consequences and effects. Judith Herman, who introduced many of us to complex trauma (Herman 1992/2022), more recently suggested, 'If traumatic disorders are afflictions of the powerless, then empowerment must be a central principle in recovery. If trauma shames and isolates, then recovery must take place in community' (Herman, 2023). She now considers Justice to be the additional (fourth) stage of recovery for survivors of trauma. Social justice, encompassing having one's experience acknowledged, together with consequent changes within the survivor's community, is as much a part of healing from complex trauma as is individual therapy.

Conclusion

In conclusion, we have made great strides in making sense of the potential effects of overwhelming or horrifying experiences on the individual. However, we now need to stride further in our understanding of the nature of complex trauma and of the process of healing. Our understanding needs to extend beyond detailed theories of intrapsychic processes to systemic approaches that also recognise the spiritual and relational impact and/or the personal and systemic need for social justice. To do otherwise is to risk the unconscious blaming of our client (once again), this time for failing to recover despite being offered the very best evidence-based therapy.

Reflection point 8.2

1 Has a client ever reported something you struggle to make sense of? (How might you explore whether this has been encountered before?)
2 What uplifts you? What makes you whole? What connects you? (How might you enquire about spirituality within your assessment?)
3 How are social justice and recovery from trauma potentially related?

Endnote

This is a commonly reported, understandable, peri-traumatic mistake (if the vehicle did not in fact catch fire) that is often triggered by seeing the fine white powder from the airbag. The powder (akin to talcum powder) is used to prevent the airbag material sticking together when tightly packed. It explodes into the vehicle cabin and continues to slowly settle, long after the airbag has deflated. This is important for people to understand as part of their development of a more contextual, verbally accessible memory of their RTA (Brewin et al., 1996; Brewin and Burgess, 2014).

Love and the relational aspect of trauma

Divine Charura, Emma Bradshaw and Mark McFetridge

Overview

This chapter will explore the different kinds of love and the relational aspect of trauma.

- We will consider why it is important to consider the concept of love when writing about trauma.
- We emphasise the importance of love and attachment in human development. We also highlight our understanding of why for some people it's much safer not to love when traumatised.
- We consider the challenges of containment and holding trauma, considering the wider context when working relationally with those who have experienced trauma.

Introduction

In this chapter we propose that the concept of trauma cannot be explored without an investigation of the importance of love and attachment. We are informed, for example, by humanistic psychology insights from Maslow's hypothesis of the hierarchy of needs, in which he noted feeling loved, accepted and belonging as one level of the hierarchy of human needs which followed physiological needs, such as safety, sustenance and shelter (Maslow, 1943). We assert in this chapter that experiences that impact our capacity for connection, belonging and safety can exacerbate experiences of trauma. Trauma happens in relationship and therefore working through relational trauma requires a therapeutic relationship in which acceptance, safety and trust can be re-established (Charura & Paul, 2015; Charura & Smith, 2023). In line with this, the humanistic psychologist Rogers, in hypothesising the theory of personality change, argued that the facilitative, key therapeutic conditions could be encapsulated as love (Rogers, 1959). This aligns with Charura and Paul's (2015) notion that love is the agent for change and that in the evaluation of the successful therapeutic engagement, love cannot be reduced 'to particular words or skills or an objectified state' (p.9). Rather, it is an authentic encounter with a quality of relating, dialogue, contact and collaborative process moment by moment in a way that fully embraces our experiences (Paul & Charura, 2014). These therapeutic qualities are essential in supporting those that present with trauma, and we will elaborate on this further within this chapter.

A note on language

We would like to acknowledge that language evolves quickly and thus in the chosen terminology in this chapter, the aim is to convey and to use language sensitively and appropriately. We foreground the importance of acknowledging the impact of language and why our values as psychologists encompass ways of seeing human beings in their diversity through a respectful, humanising and valuing way. We are committed to using language in a culturally sensitive way and in exploring the concept of love and trauma we also bring recognition of the traumatic experiences, fragility of identity and discrimination experienced by minoritised groups. Furthermore, we highlight that love as a verb requires action and therefore we illuminate the value of anti-discriminatory practice and are informed by principles which guide socio-political action within and beyond the therapy room. This includes, for example, engaging with the question 'Where is the love in the world?' in relation to the experiences of those who suffer the impact of being othered, social injustice, human rights violations and a progressive vision for socio-political change (Tribe & Charura, 2023).

Why consider the concept of love when writing about trauma?

In our discussion of whether love has a place in working with trauma, we begin here by concurring with Gupta (2022) who conceptualised an existential rights paradigm for anti-oppressive practice which is centred on truth, freedom, love, hope and exploration of power discourses (Cosgrove & Shaughnessy, 2020; Gupta, 2022; Tribe & Charura, 2023).

An important place to start for those who critique the concept of love in trauma work is to refer to the right to love by acknowledging the need for all human beings to belong to a community (Gupta, 2022). In line with this, Tribe and Charura (2023) argued for love and social justice as human rights. We also concur with the existential psychologist Erich Fromm's (1956) definition of love which incapsulates an attitude and orientation toward the whole world, enacted through caring actions that promote others' growth and wellbeing (Fromm, 1956; Smith, 2020). Furthermore, in considering the concept of love from a therapeutic context, Thorne (2012) argued for 'a view of human nature and relationality which highlighted the importance of acknowledging spiritual accompaniment perspectives that focus on the qualities of tenderness and presence, and love in the therapeutic encounter' (Thorne, 2012). There is also a plethora of writers who have argued for what has been termed 'therapeutic love or love in humanity in the highest sense of agape'. *Agape* is not an unethical love which transgresses boundaries but rather an encapsulation of the facilitative conditions for therapy/encounter. This includes the powerful dynamics experienced through compassion, positive regard of the humanity of the individual/group or community, empathy, warmth and acceptance of other/s (Charura & Paul, 2015; Patterson, 1974; van Deurzen, 2015). An expansion of the concept of experiencing agape, and the depth of connection experienced in therapy includes deep participation with, and acceptance of, another's essential being termed by the philosopher Martin Buber as the 'I-thou' relationship (Buber, 2008), while others have coined the term 'relational depth' to describe deep moments of encounter within the therapeutic context (Knox et al., 2013). Although we do not have space in this chapter to expand further on all the therapeutic roots or critique of the concept of 'love' when working with individuals in therapeutic individual, group and community contexts, we wanted to highlight love firstly from a human rights perspective. We also acknowledge that, particularly when working with trauma, this conceptualisation is also fraught with caution due to potential unethical practice and abuse that can emerge from it. Through our practice we have learnt that many clients and patients who present with trauma may have had traumatic experiences such as abuse, all resulting from acts perpetrated in the name of what may have been wrongly labelled as 'love'.

Importance of love and attachment

Another area we refer to is the importance of love and the impact of its absence on the human psyche (as discussed by Charura & Paul, 2015). The importance of love and attachments within primary relationships, which provide the foundation for the evolution of co-operative behaviours and connection in relation to children's mental and physical wellbeing, is well documented (Bowlby, 1969; Gerhardt, 2015). This mutual drive towards interdependence, relationship and connection is a biological necessity and the very foundation of intersubjectivity and the capacity for empathy (Charura & Paul, 2015). Attachment patterns formed in infancy also influence how individuals respond when faced with trauma or challenges later in life. The way in which an infant is parented impacts upon the social and emotional development, capacity to adjust behaviours and emotional regulation (Bornstein et al., 2018). Lack of love and a nurturing relationship in childhood affects the development of neurological pathways in the brain, and many studies have shown in the worst cases that children have died because of lack of love, relational trauma and absence of nurturing relationships (Mikulincer & Florian, 2000; Mikulincer & Shaver, 2016).

We do, however, note that the most significant aspect of the conceptualisation of the right to love – whether in therapeutic or community contexts – is respect. In this chapter our assertion is that love is relayed through actions which portray respect of the others' difference and are demonstrated through our humanity towards them. In consequence, we demonstrate our awareness of their unique individuality through anti-discriminatory practice and authentic encounter (Fromm, 1956; Smith, 2020).

What has love got to do with trauma?

Despite the evidence of the impact of the absence of love within diverse literature, it is difficult to define what it is. Watts and Stenner (2014) identified the importance of Barthes' (1990) claim that love cannot be defined by a singular theory of love and that any attempts to define love should focus on a concern about its affirmation and what people say and do in love's name (Barthes, 1990). Figure 9.1 shows, in summary, eight different kinds of love as noted in the literature that we have scoped (Lee, 1977; van Deurzen, 2015; Watts & Stenner, 2014).

Figure 9.1 Different kinds of love and potential for trauma

Athenian love	Potential areas of trauma which clients may present with
1. **Agape,** unconditional, divine or mystical love.	Some clients may present with religious trauma, and some may also find Agape through faith, spirituality, therapy and healing.
2. **Storge,** which is parental love for their children.	Some clients we work with often present with trauma from childhood and traumatic experiences arising from abuse or neglect from parents or primary care givers.
3. **Philia,** the love felt in companionship in a community.	Trauma can also be experienced through marginalisation and discrimination in communities.
4. **Eros,** sensual, sexual or erotic love, often also associated with passion, lust or desire.	Trauma in relation to eros may have been experienced through sexual, romantic or intimate relationships. Trauma may also have been experienced through trusting loving relationships that violated the boundary of trust (i.e., through infidelity, betrayal, traumatic separation or divorce). It could also be through masquerades of 'I love you', wrong justifications stating, 'we are in a relationship' and abusing the other. Sexual abuse or rape are also causes of trauma that individuals we support present with.
5. **Ludus,** game-playing love (Playful Interactions: Uncommitted Love)	Ludus love can result in trauma experienced through game playing sexual, pseudo-romantic, relational flings and relationships.

Figure 9.1 (*continued*)

6. **Narcissism,** which others have debated to be a negative and selfish kind of self-love.	Narcissism presentations may be a creative adjustment to childhood trauma, meaning that someone may develop narcissistic tendencies as a defence to childhood trauma or neglect. Another point is that the impact of being on the receiving end of narcissistic behaviour over time may be traumatic. For example, the impact of a narcissistic parent or partner may be traumatic.
7. **Xenia,** the love of strangers or neighbours in hospitality.	Trauma can arise from harm from strangers or discrimination and not being welcome in communities, for example, when seeking asylum. However, receiving love from strangers and neighbours can also be healing and restorative.
8. **Pragma,** which is (Storge + Ludus) realistic and practical Love.	Realistic and practical love may be a creative adjustment or defence which helps individuals to manage through living with trauma.

It is important to consider reflexively the view of love from the perspective of those presenting with trauma; each embodying their own experience and holding their own interpretation of the meaning of love, which will be influenced by embodied early relational contact and experiences, their sense of mattering, external observations of love through media and the examination of love in others (Sternberg & Sternberg, 2019). Furthermore, cultural values, whether collectivist or individualistic, will influence the precise meaning that is attributed to the term *love*.

It's much safer to not love when traumatised: a reflection on our clinical cases

In our discussions about love and trauma in writing this book, we questioned why it can often be so difficult for those presenting with trauma to engage in relationships and to love. As psychologists, we have all known of individuals who have died following serious trauma, such as, for example, traumatic grief. We therefore concur with the assertion that we are all born in relationships and develop through relationships, and without love our brain limbic systems atrophy (weakening of neurones) (Charura & Paul, 2015; Gerhardt, 2015).

The therapeutic relationship is about intimacy as clients and patients often bring their most personal experiences of trauma. In working with our clients, such as those presented through our case studies in Chapter 4, it is evident to us that all our clients noted in our case studies struggled with relationships and accepting love following their experiences of trauma. Farrokh, for example, described an out-of-body body experience while being tortured and he described having spiritual visions of some of his family who had died many years ago. He described that this betray of trust by 'his own people who tortured him', meant that he did not trust anyone any more and could not have a relationship as he had 'nothing left to give'.

In the cases of both Little V and Willow, part of their individual therapies was to work through their defences and creative adjustments of dissociating in moments of intimacy. All of us as psychologists and therapists had to also work through with these clients in the psychosexual domain, by supporting the clients through their sexual difficulties including for example erectile dysfunction, vaginismus, extreme anxiety and avoidance of relational and sexual intimacy. We also want to highlight here that not all trauma leads to difficulties in sexual functioning and that we are aware of clients who have shared narratives of sexual promiscuity also arising from trauma. It is therefore important to note that each client's presentation is different; what we assert here is that each presentation is unique and that the therapist should be aware of the impact of trauma within the different domains, including the sexual impact. We draw again here from O'Brien and Charura (2023) whose description of *embodied trauma* notes that it is the whole body's response to a significant traumatic event, where mental distress is experienced within the body as a physiological, psychological, biological, cultural or relational reaction to trauma. They suggest that in working with trauma (and for us in this chapter in relation to love), it is important to encompass a holistic approach which covers bio-psycho-social-sexual-spiritual-existential presentations (O'Brien & Charura, 2023).

While from different therapeutic orientations we can attempt to conceptualise these experiences, what is often important for clients is to be heard and listened to as they engage in therapy and explore potential meanings of their experiences and trauma. It is also important to focus on this in supervision to ensure that cultural, spiritual or religious conceptualisations for psychological distress and healing are not ignored, as they carry meaning for those we support.

In the case of Farrokh (a client noted in one of our case studies in Chapter 4), for example, through therapeutic presence he was able to work though his trauma. The loving presence in the work of intimacy is not about 'loving the client' as an intellectual act, but this is about valuing their humanity with all the ugliness that they have been through and accepting them for who they are. In our discussions we discussed that the word intimacy can be viewed as symbolic of the phrase 'into-me-see'. This level of depth and vulnerability with each other (between therapist and client) is a kind of openness with other on a very deep psychic, emotional and spiritual level. What we are referring to here is not an unethical reference to intimacy; for example, your therapist violating your boundaries as a client, for instance, by sleeping with you or breaking the boundary of the therapeutic relationship through engaging in activities that are devaluing. Rather, in other words, the love that we are making reference to here is akin to an 'agape' kind of love which includes the powerful dynamics experienced through compassion, positive regard of the humanity of the individual/group or community, empathy, warmth and acceptance of other/s (Charura & Paul, 2015; van Deurzen, 2015).

In our reflections on experiences of trauma that the clients presented in our case studies, and that many clients we have worked with bring to therapy, we note that their experiences, while all labelled or understood by them as trauma, could mean so many different things. Thus, for therapists, the work is journeying with the client through not just the specific traumatic event that caused/continues to cause them pain, but also often through their story of the absence of love that would have perpetuated their pain. An example is that an individual could have been abused by their father and that would have been wrong, traumatic and distressing; a part of their trauma, however, could have been the fact that they knew that their mother was in the house hearing their cries and not intervening. It could have also been that the trusted adults such as others in the family, or at school, who might have intervened or asked did not. With this understanding, we assert that from a therapeutic commitment perspective, what the therapist then offers in place of this absence of love is a commitment on the therapist's part to be present, to listen, to act/be prepared to act (i.e., take appropriate safeguarding steps where these emerge) each week without fail, pursuing their attempts to help the client to work through the trauma. The therapist's commitment is to be present within the therapeutic encounter in the sacred space of therapy, holding the boundary and frame of therapy. This enables the working through of the trauma, through the offer of an ethical professional therapeutic relationship, love, compassion, respect of the client/couple/family or community and offers an emotionally corrective experience (Paul & Charura, 2014).

The challenges of containment and holding trauma

In the writing of this chapter, we discussed the impact of holding and containing the client's experiences of trauma and transference. We concur that the dynamic of working with traumatic material includes dealing with projection of fear onto the therapist. We have worked with colleagues who relayed the extreme impact of containing such projections.

One therapist who was working with refugees and asylum seekers stated to one of us (the first author DC) that:

> umm... I remember sitting with one mum and she suddenly screamed and was seeing people coming out of this cupboard, so much so that I went, and I checked the cupboard darling ... which was silly..., really.... because I had kept materials for art therapy for 20 years.... well, it wasn't silly for her, but I suddenly thought...., Oh god what if there is somebody in the cupboard but that's a knock-on effect of working with serious Trauma. (Charura, 2024)

In another context, the second author (MF) remembered giving supervision to a colleague whose supervision sessions for a while focused on working out what was real and what was not. They stated that their whole sense of confusion was working through in supervision what had been projected into/onto them through working with clients presenting with trauma. These experiences relay the importance of self-care, and the importance of therapists coping with the inevitable impact of the work, to ensure that they have opportunities to debrief and to be able to function outside of work so enabling them to keep doing the work.

We also note here the importance of paying attention to the psycho-spiritual aspects of trauma. As psychologists who for many years have worked with individuals, couples and families presenting with trauma, we have reflected on many experiences in which clients accessing therapy for trauma may have had religious conceptualisations of their trauma or the trauma may be seen as a spiritual emergence. This attention to individuals' or communities' faith, spiritual conceptualisations or containing perspectives of healing, which may encapsulate love, is important for therapists to hold in their formulations and discussions with those they work with.

At times it may be that in working with trauma we also face experiences which are scientifically inexplicable. In writing this book we shared many narratives of experiences in which we worked with clients and patients who shared experiences of being ritualistically abused. Some described trauma in which they had had near-death experiences, resulting in transformation of their life perspective. At times, experiences through/in therapy can be a challenge to understand. For example, in one case we discussed one of us hearing a narrative of clients in group therapy witnessing 'something' – described as 'a mystical figure' jump from a distressed client, 'right into the therapist'. The group therapist also at the same time became distressed and voiced that they experienced a metaphysical experience of being invaded. Now this is one of many examples of narratives that relay spiritual, or scientifically inexplicable, experiences that have been shared with us by clients, and patients, in therapy relating to trauma as well as by therapists in supervision. Our aim, however, is not to explain these in this chapter but rather to illuminate the importance of those working with trauma being aware of the potential spiritual dimension of trauma and its impact on these presenting in the consultation room or in community.

In some of our work we have learnt of traditional trauma healing practices that include removing 'objects' from within the body of the patients presenting to the traditional healer with trauma. While these experiences may be understood from different epistemologies, such as Islamic or African psychology, they manifest a reality for clients we work with that challenges us as clinicians to think and explore how we paint narratives of treating trauma from a Eurocentric psychotherapeutic lens. In our discussions we understood the importance of therapists not only containing experiences and narratives that are different to those from their own cultural or spiritual orientation their own but also being open to learn more as part of their own development.

While we speak above of different epistemologies and their conceptualisation of embodied trauma and healing practices, we also did however find similarities from Freud's early writing on the embodied manifestation of trauma. For example, consider Freud's work in which he hypothesised a human being's inability to conceal unconscious material, when he stated:

> When I set myself the task of bringing to light what human beings keep hidden with him…I thought the task was a harder one than it really is. He that has eyes to see and ears to hear may convince himself that no mortal can keep a secret. If his lips are silent, he chatters with his finger-tips; betrayal oozes out of him at every pore. (Freud, 1953, p.77)

In this quote we understood that holding and suppressing traumatic experiences for a client has a psychological impact as the disturbance of the traumatic experience/s seeks a way from the hidden into the surface of consciousness or manifestation through somatic/bodily or psychological dis-ease. Thus, the work of trauma therapy is to work with the client and to bring into consciousness, hold and contain that which the client may be struggling to deal with or make sense of in relation to their experiences of trauma.

The importance of holding and containment of the client

The interpersonal/relational, intrapsychic experiences and reactions generated by listening to the trauma, with empathy, love, attunement and compassion to the client's traumatic material, impacts the therapist. It is therefore important that as therapists we pay attention to our therapeutic vulnerability and seek support as well as engaging in self-care to ensure that we are also held and contained (Paul & Charura 2014). Here we reflect on the importance of the concepts of holding and the holding environment (Winnicott, 1960) and containing (Bion, 1962). In Winnicottian terms, 'holding' originally derives from the maternal care-taking function of providing the infant and child with a sense of safety and protection (of being held). It is used metaphorically in therapeutic terms to refer to aspects of the therapeutic process in which the therapist conveys in words the client's deep anxiety and trauma and becomes the receptacle for the client's unbearable split-off affects, thus increasing a capacity for the client to tolerate and work through the traumatic material. Alongside this, we draw on Bion's (1962) concept of containing emotions, which does not mean compartmentalising or controlling them, but rather an opening up by the therapist as a container to allow for psychic space for the client to pour out the destabilising traumatic poison from themselves. In line with this, Charura and Bushell (2023) asserted that for healing, it is necessary that the traumatic material does emerge and become conscious and that, in such moments, the art of the therapist is to hold the poison, know it and yet not use it to harm the client, (for example when the client may repeat a pattern such as engaging in behaviours that may seem unhelpful to themselves); but instead it is important for the therapist to see the health in the venom by recognising it as a manifestation of traumatic energy and to explore ways of engaging with it for transformation and change (Charura & Bushell, 2023). Through the act of loving the other as they are –listening and respecting them as a human being doing their best, moment by moment trying to work through trauma, working with whatever emerges or is shared in the therapeutic space–material is contained and held in conscious awareness, bringing about a breaking down to the original traumatic component.

Experiences of trauma may also mean that clients find it difficult to love or to feel loved, or to engage in intimate or sexual encounters. So van Deurzen's (2015) perspectives on work with love apply in this context as she argued that, in working with such existential challenges, we carefully consider how a person loves and relates and enable them to open up to a more complete way of loving. Instead of focusing on the desire of wanting 'to be loved', focus should be on exploring how a person loves.

It has also been noted that it is important for the therapist to remain both visible and present in the consulting room and at the same time have the capacity to hold and self-contain their own subjective material, experiences and responses to (transference-countertransference enactments) the dynamics that emerge in the intersubjective space between them and the client presenting with trauma. Here we are again turning to the work of the existentialist Emmy van Deurzen (2015) who reminds us that if to love someone is to let them be and live as fully and freely as possible, keeping their welfare at heart, in a dedicated, attentive and uncompromising way as therapists, then this should be an important concept to us. That is, within a therapeutic concept to see the other as what they are capable of being-becoming rather than only as what they were in the past, or what they are now in light of their trauma experience. Van Deurzen (2015) argues that this is the hallmark of an *I–Thou* way of relating as this way of being opens the relationship to the future and moves it beyond actuality towards potentiality. This is what we might call cherishing a person: that is, actively keeping their wellbeing in mind and promoting it, even though this will often be demanding and challenging.

Conclusion

We conclude here with the reflection that what we are referring to as 'love' in this therapeutic context, far from just being a feeling that we experience or unethical acts of pursuing our own desires, is, rather, an action, a way of being, a commitment, an attitude of care, that is wholly about a particular kind of intentionality, a movement towards valuing, prizing and deeply respecting the humanity of the other and their process of becoming. This enables us to be in therapeutic encounter and to dialogue and have responsibility (*response-ability*) to work through the trauma and, all the time, engaging in learning about the other's experience and what it means to really be with other human beings.

Reflection point 9.1

1 What are your reflections on how the role of love has changed over time in the psychological professions and therapeutic work?
2 What theories may help you to conceptualise and critique the concept of love in trauma therapy?
3 Reflect on the clients you have worked with and on your own experiences: what do you need to challenge and consider in your practice and supervision in relation to love, transference, diversity and working with trauma?

10 Contemporary systemic perspectives of trauma

Mark McFetridge, Emma Bradshaw and Divine Charura

Overview
- This chapter considers systemic perspectives of trauma, including working with couples, families and communities.
- We highlight a relational understanding of the impact of trauma.
- We emphasise a consideration of the uniqueness of each context when formulating an individual's traumatic experience.

Introduction

'It takes a village to raise a child.'

This old proverb derives from Ubuntu, the African philosophy of humanism or 'humble togetherness' which links an individual to the collective through brotherhood or sisterhood (Swanson, 2008). Ubuntu points to the contribution of a system of people within and beyond our immediate family and the importance of this as we develop and grow, and beyond this, go about our daily living. Many of us, unfamiliar with this proverb, may consider it to be outdated. However, the proverb may still be valid if given a contemporary interpretation (Reupert et al., 2022). It may also remind us how, in many Western cultures, we have become distant from an appreciation of the influence of our wider system as we have become increasingly individual-focused.

But what of our time of crisis, and when we need to heal and recover? Surely if our system is important for our growth then it is also important for our healing? Some have suggested that the key agent of change of psychological therapies is not the individual insight or skills acquired, but rather the enabling capacity these newfound skills provide us to engage effectively with our 'village' (BBC, 2020; see *Key resources and further reading*). It is our new or regained ability to engage with other people, to ask for help and offer help to others, that provides sustained healing and the promise of good mental health.

It is possible that psychological therapy may be merely the catalyst for achieving this sustaining systemic change.

The therapeutic community

One therapeutic approach that has embodied this relational focus, perhaps more than any other, is the therapeutic community (TC). The historic Belgian town of Geel has been credited as one of the earliest known forms of this community approach to mental health. In the sixth century CE, a young woman escaped from Ireland across the sea to Geel after refusing the inappropriate demands of her father for her to replace her deceased mother. Dymphna was followed by her father, King Damon, and his men and eventually discovered in the Geel chapel where she had sought sanctuary. However, she chose to be beheaded there rather than return with her father and yield to his wish. In the years that followed, the chapel became associated with miraculous cures of 'madness'. In 1247, she was canonised as Saint Dymphna, the patron saint of the mentally ill, and the mentally ill of Europe flocked to Geel (Goldstein & Godemont, 2003). The struggling pilgrims, now overwhelming the hospital accommodation, were increasingly taken in and looked after by the local town folk. These spontaneous acts of kindness of the Geel villagers became a tradition of truly integrated community residential care that continues to this day.

Some say, '*It takes a woman*' (Agyeman-Rawlings, 2018); in 1792 this young woman was Ann Tuke, a York Quaker. After hearing of the death of a young widow in the York Asylum, Anne asked her father, William Tuke, why the Quakers couldn't have a hospital for their own society of friends. William went on to petition the York meeting of Quakers for such an institution, for those who 'laboured under that most afflictive dispensation; the loss of reason'. Anne had sowed the seed of what was to become the Retreat, York, later credited as the first residential therapeutic community (Haigh & Pearce, 2017). The Retreat was reported to have achieved 'marked amelioration of the condition of the insane' by simply rejecting the inhumane interventions of the day and adopting 'kindness and judicious treatment'.

More recently, the therapeutic community has been described as a form of therapeutic environment which includes five essential psychosocial elements (Haigh, 2013):

- attachment: a culture of belonging
- containment: a culture of safety
- communication: a culture of openness
- involvement and inclusion: a culture of participation and citizenship
- agency: a culture of empowerment.

Through the participation of both clients and staff members in the living–learning processes of the community, Haigh (2013) suggests that secondary emotional development is possible, i.e. therapeutic change, for those whose childhoods and primary emotional development had been lacking in these factors.

Latterly, the Retreat developed a TC for women with histories of severe self-defeating behaviour, and again demonstrated notable clinical outcomes in people with complex mental health needs and histories. These personal and relational gains were found to be not only evident during conventional short-er-term periods of evaluation, but were also reported on follow-up at 3, 6 and 9 years later (McFetridge & Coakes, 2010). While this specialist UK-wide service was commissioned by the NHS for people meeting diagnostic criteria for bor-derline personality disorder (American Psychiatric Association, 2022), it was found that 75 per cent of these women also had previously documented reported histories of childhood sexual abuse (McFetridge et al., 2015).

Ecological systems

As practitioner psychologists, much of what we focus on is directly from the individual by whose side we sit, and from their personal experience to which we attend and respect. While this is of fundamental importance in our work, it is not the only thing we need to consider. Something we may find saddening about our traumatised clients is how commonly they may demonstrate a perva-sive bias in their making sense of events in the form of a creative self-blaming. If we are not careful to actively recognise and reclaim our own responsibility, they may even blame themselves for our own mistakes.

One potential reason for this attributional bias to self-blame is that pri-mary carers and/or others have unintentionally negatively influenced our client's schemas, primary cognitions or conditions of worth during their childhood. However, this negative attributional bias may sometimes, sadly, be influenced by deliberate intent. Many years ago, I (MM) learned from col-leagues working within sex offender services, that we should also consider the possibility that what a survivor of childhood abuse believes may be what the perpetrator *wanted* them to believe. This may be part of the 'grooming' process of the abuse, and in some cases is carefully engineered. There may be many reasons for this victim blaming, but one evident possibility is that self-blame and the consequent secrecy and feelings of shame significantly reduce the risk of anyone else being informed of the abuse.

It is much easier to look back and see past social influences than to be aware of the systemic influences currently active upon, and around, us. However, it is likely to be helpful to take time to work with our clients to consider their sys-tems and incorporate this into a shared formulation of their difficulties. One model that may assist with this was offered by Bronfenbrenner (2000), as seen in Figure 10.1.

The ecological systems theory proposed that, rather than an individual sim-ply being surrounded by a series of concentric circles representing levels of influence (microsystem; mesosystem; exosystem; macrosystem; chronosys-tem), we are in fact in synergistic interaction with these. In other words, we are

Figure 10.1 Bronfenbrenner's ecological model

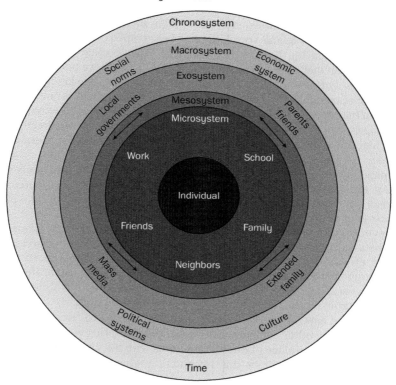

Source: **Created by and reproduced with the kind permission of Olivia Guy-Evans from Simply Psychology.**

influenced by our environment, culture and systems, and in turn we interact with and influence these. Bronfenbrenner later renamed this the *Bioecological model* to underline the biological differences between us and within us over time, which influence the ways in which this dynamic (two-way) interaction occurs with our systems. Our sex, skin colour, height and weight are but a few examples of the biological aspects of ourselves that influence how we relate to our microsystem, and how all levels of the systems relate to us.

The digital virtual world

The bioecological model was further developed to incorporate our contemporary digital world (Navarro & Tudge, 2023) on the reasonable premise that this may also have a systemic influence upon us. The extent of this will vary between us, but many of us know only too well the addictive effect of our engagement with social media. Navarro and Tudge (2023) suggested the microsystem may now comprise both physical and virtual systems; this is perhaps of particular significance for currently developing adolescents and our potential understanding of them. The recent frontiers of this digital virtual microsystem are virtual reality (VR) and artificial intelligence (AI). Sadly, there are already numerous reports of the avatars of female social VR users being raped or sexually assaulted; being predated upon by those waiting for new unsuspecting and vulnerable adventurers in the metaverse (Schulenberg et al., 2023). These authors suggest that the virtual world is further accentuating the normative world's harassment and discrimination against women in the USA, particularly Black women.

The fully immersive nature of the live-streamed, interactive VR experienced by our senses seems startlingly real. The entertainment and recreational value of VR is already well known, but could this also be harnessed for therapeutic purposes?

The psychotherapeutic potential of VR for the treatment of individuals with psychosis has been reported (Freeman et al., 2023), and beneficial outcomes have also been demonstrated for people with PTSD (Deng et al., 2019; Kothgassner et al., 2019).

However, if VR is sufficiently powerful to facilitate therapeutic gains, we need to be aware that it could also facilitate harm, and potentially also lead to traumatic effects. I (MM) recall a client some 30 years ago reporting his traumatising experience of a 'bad trip' with his first, and only, use of the hallucinogenic substance LSD. He felt petrified and powerless within a compelling and unpredictable world, far beyond the remit of his normality.

In our clinical assessments, it would therefore be wise to remain alert and open to considering other contemporary forms of traumatic events and enquire about our client's experience of their interactions with the virtual microsystem. Our clients may not volunteer this information; shame is able to virtually silence us, too.

The impact of trauma on the family system

The secondary effect of an individual's trauma on their family members is well known from the early studies of survivors of the Holocaust during the Second World War, 1939–1945, and from research with their children (Shuval, 1957). We referred earlier to the effects of transgenerational trauma, in Chapter 3. This phenomenon was explored by Scharf (2007), in their extensive examination of the systemic and intergenerational effects on the second and third generations of holocaust survivors. It was found that the adult children of families in which there was one holocaust survivor parent functioned as well as those without holocaust family experience. This was also the case for their adolescent grandchildren. However, a different picture emerged for the children and grandchildren where both partners had been holocaust survivors. Their adolescent grandchildren described their mothers and fathers as less accepting and encouraging of their independence. The grandchildren had less positive self-perceptions and a higher level of ambivalent (insecure) attachment. Scharf (2007) recommended we enquire of our clients about the potential traumatic experiences of their parents and grandparents as part of our routine assessments.

Clearly, there will be different consequences for the traumatised individual within their immediate system, depending on whether details of their experience are known. If family members are aware of what our client has endured, it is likely that there is a different understanding and related responses compared to when there is an absence of such knowledge. There may be a wish to prevent any further distress for the traumatised family member by avoiding reference to, or acknowledgement of, what happened. The unintended consequence of this may be that their traumatised relative feels their experience, and the effect of this, is disregarded. Perhaps in addition, feelings of distress and guilt experienced by parents that terrible events have happened to their child, may compromise their usual capacity to effectively contain and nurture them.

For many traumatised people, their traumatic memories have an insidiously isolating effect. This may be due to a fear of losing control of emotion in public and the imagined social disgrace of this, or the direct energy-sapping effect of interrupted sleep, poor concentration and sustained emotional arousal. Additionally, the trauma, particularly if interpersonal, may entail shame rather than fear as the predominant experienced emotion. Whatever the reason for our shame, this primitive, primary emotion drives us to look down and avoid eye contact, perhaps in fear that we may see our shame reflected in the eyes of others. We have evolved as social animals with a primitive fear of being ostracised. However, these social consequences of trauma are likely to be experienced differently, particularly by some neurodiverse people and their families, and will therefore require careful exploration and assessment beyond these normative assumptions.

Working with trauma within couples, families and communities

As a clinician, our flexibility to offer anything broader than individual input will vary with the real-world constraints of our workplace setting. However, in reality, our work and the relational context for this is more dynamic than this suggests when considered over time. Where we contribute from within a team, our appetite for unfamiliar ways of working, for containing uncertainty and our levels of creativity, may co-vary with the level of team cohesion at any given time. This is again dynamic, however, and potentially enhanced with our input.

Considering the context of the inpatient psychiatric hospital system, a range of potential multi-level contributions has been outlined of the practitioner psychologist (McFetridge, 2019). Additional roles may include the facilitation of a psychologically minded team (able to adopt a stance of therapeutic curiosity); acting as a culture carrier to new colleagues within the ward team; acting as a researcher and scientist-practitioner (to evaluate the service and disseminate clinical outcomes); acting as a trainer of the team; and, finally, as a provider of informal leadership and enhancing emotional containment. These contributions complement the perhaps more familiar roles of individual and group therapy facilitation.

Considering the outpatient setting, a way of engaging the client's immediate system that I (MM) have found helpful has been to see the traumatised individual alone initially for assessment then, with permission, invite partners to the second half of a further (subsequent) assessment session. This has then been repeated as therapy progresses, and at review or transitional sessions. It is often informative to hear the perspective of a loved one or friend of our client, and to be able to observe their relating. In addition, their involvement potentially prepares the way for a supportive and understanding system around our client during later active trauma processing. One of the issues it can be important to explain to partners is that, during the stage of actively addressing the trauma, it may appear as if our client is 'getting worse'. In fact, this is the predictable (and temporary) effect of this phase of the therapy and its rekindling of the traumatic memory and script. The systemic intervention here, therefore, is assisting their partner to be able to recognise this change in functioning of our client when it occurs, enabling them to support and contain, and not inadvertently react to any distress unhelpfully. Sometimes it has also been helpful, if the client agrees, to invite their partner in to participate in a mid-therapy review. Again, this potentially assists the client's immediate system to contain and support their therapeutic process and change.

When once I was referred a traumatised couple who had been in a serious accident together, I (MM) had to consider what was the most effective thing to do. Despite injuries they had survived the same life-threatening accident together but would be expected to have differing experience of this, not least as driver and as passenger. At this stage it was also important to be aware that there may be issues of blame, responsibility and anger between the partners, and this could require sensitivity, if not confidentiality, to be acknowledged. However, why not arrive at a decision and plan with the couple themselves? (It was clearly a more creative day for me, and at a time I felt well-supported by colleagues.) So I opted to meet them together, assess them as a couple and arrive together at a decision of how we would proceed. It was agreed I would start with individual sessions with the female partner and offer EMDR on her experience of being a passenger. Furthermore, we would review regularly together with her male partner, before reversing this with him as the focus. I went on to offer trauma therapy with the male partner, with reviews together with his now recovered partner. While the couple decided on this, perhaps traditional and chivalrous, order of our therapeutic work, what I had not anticipated was the significant added therapeutic benefit of subsequent reviews together with his partner who had now worked through her traumatic experience and knew the process and the benefit of doing so.

Many systemic family therapists, as we might anticipate, consider forms of mental health difficulty as residing in the interactions and thinking of the family system. Their client is the family as a whole, a dynamic entity in its own right. A comprehensive review of the various systemic models is beyond our immediate scope; however, the interested reader is directed to Catherall (2013) who reviewed the theoretical models and approaches to family intervention potentially helpful to the traumatised family. This included consideration of a contextual approach, object relations and emotionally focused and critical interaction therapies.

The collective trauma of communities

Let us now consider the example of when the whole system is affected by a traumatic event. Saul (2022) considered the multiple effects of individual traumatic events on families and communities and noted the potential effects of collective trauma as particularly severe. Collective trauma can affect a family and community following disasters that have commonly entailed both the traumatic loss of life and loss of family resources, or following the cumulative effect of poverty, illness displacement and oppression. The intervention suggested (Saul, 2022) is one of collective approaches to readjustment and resilience of the family, and the strengthening of the community through creative and flexible multi-level attention to the system.

It can be challenging (if not deeply unsettling) for those of us more used to individual work to have to consider how we would intervene helpfully beyond the safe space within the therapy room walls. If we found ourselves without an office, and alongside a significant number of potentially traumatised people, what might we do to help, and how might we best offer some form of psychological intervention?

One form of trauma therapy detailed earlier (Chapter 7), has been found to be particularly suited to adaptation for use within communities. Bedard-Gilligan et al. (2022) describe their use of NET (narrative exposure therapy) as a focus for some tribal communities of American-Indian people. This entailed a series of stages of work with the community. A partnership was first formed incorporating community leaders, therapy providers and participants to engage in the process of arriving at, and delivering, a form of NET appropriately adapted for the specific community. These established modifications included a focus on historical and intergenerational trauma, enhanced confidentiality necessary for a small community, and the inclusion of important cultural traditions and customs. The authors concluded that not only was the therapy delivered itself effective, but the entire process of collaboratively developing the appropriate local adaptations to NET as a community intervention was helpful and should be similarly implemented in other close-knit community settings (Bedard-Gilligan et al., 2022).

The use of narrative exposure therapy was further explored within traumatised communities of the Eastern Democratic Republic of Congo, following the armed conflict of 1998–2004, in which at least a million people were killed (Kapend et al., 2020). This intervention notably included the processing together as a community of not only their experiences of suffering violence, but also their experiences of perpetrating violence (Schmitt et al., 2022). Attitudes improved towards these ex-combatants who had inflicted harm, as did the perceived social acknowledgement after trauma. There were improvements in PTSD symptoms for NET participants, and the rejection of previous unhelpful community myths about rape. Change in community-held beliefs resulted from the community intervention of collating and distributing information derived from the process of NET and from the testimonies of the trauma survivors (termed *NET-Facts*). The authors concluded this system of community-based intervention serves to share and prompt the processing of previously avoided collectively relevant facts about trauma. Otherwise, the collective avoidance of the trauma, it is suggested, accelerates the cycles of violence in these post-conflict regions of the world by protecting the perpetrators and marginalising the victims. Conversely, giving voice offers the potential of adopting new perspectives, social reapproach and reconciliation (Schmitt et al., 2022).

One of the aims of this community-focused work is to help break the familiar cycle of violence seen across the world, and repeated over time, whereby the victims' community avenge the violence perpetrated upon them by perpetrating yet further violence. These studies represent inspiring accounts of the innovative and collaborative work of practitioner psychologists to empower communities in some of the materially poorest parts of our world. Perhaps, however, the capacity and willingness of these communities to face their collective trauma, to reflect on their diverse experience of this, and to heal together, is something that might enrich us all.

Formulating our client's trauma within their context

Let us consider an alternative systemic perspective: that trauma is not an individual problem but, rather, is a social problem. Trauma is often interpersonal and perpetrated by another, may be colluded with by silent others, and unheard by wider society and those in power. This may seem an extreme perspective, however many survivors of abuse and other traumatic events consider aspects of this to resonate with their experience. Consider some of the social and political issues making headlines at the time of our writing: the UK government has been compelled to compensate those (remaining) survivors who were knowingly infected with AIDS and Hepatitis-C in the 1980s by transfusions and treatments with infected blood products. It is now over seven years since the 2017 Grenfell fire in which 72 people lost their lives. There are still many people living within similar high-rise blocks with similar dangerous cladding. In January 2024 the Fire Brigades Union warned of 'criminal complacency on the part of the government and some building firms' after a further cladding fire in London. It seems that some risks are indeed known from the traumatic consequences of previous events, but for some reason we are unable as a society to resolve these to prevent the event from repeating. Contrast these delays with the achievement of a new Covid-19 vaccine being both created and administered to most of the UK population at greatest risk, within 12 months. It is truly inspiring what we can achieve when we are determined to do so; it is equally sobering how disconnected we can be from the plight of others.

With potential contextual influences in mind, are we therefore in danger of 'missing the point' when sitting with our client (formerly little) V, and trying our best to psychotherapeutically address her traumatic memories? If we formulate her traumatic experiences and difficulties within the context of the systems around her, might we better appreciate why her traumatic symptoms appear so resistant to change? Although V has a supportive partner, she has been unable to share with him about her history of grooming and abuse by the local drug dealers. The drug dealers, unknown to her partner, continue to threaten V in order to secure her continued silence. The authorities are aware of the drug dealers threatening V and others but are more focused on bringing the major drug suppliers to justice. It also appears that the wider community turns away from reports of the abuse of teenage girls by the drug-dealing networks, rationalising it as unwise teenage relationship choices, exaggeration or 'not my problem'. Given this systemic context, how could we expect V to recover from her traumatised state?

Judith Herman (2023) suggested there is a fourth stage of treatment that is required for complete recovery from trauma, and that is one of justice. She highlights the need repeatedly expressed within her interviews of adult survivors of gender-based trauma, for *acknowledgement* (Herman, 2023). Consequently, she emphasises a need for active involvement of a further group, the bystanders, who make up the community and the institutions; that the community might stand with the victim, and in order that the one who harms is not protected to continue harming others.

This would indeed speak of social justice; however, if we are to be effective in achieving change it is important to understand the factors that make this change difficult. The long-established justice system in the UK was not designed to address the needs of survivors of interpersonal and or sexual trauma, but rather to establish the guilt or (continued) innocence of the alleged perpetrator. The requirement of a fair trial for those accused of a crime cannot and should not be overridden; however, the legal process relating to gender-based and interpersonal violence urgently needs to improve. Many, if not most, allegations do not have the opportunity to proceed to trial due to the assessed probability (by the Crown Prosecution Service) of reaching a conviction. Systems are required that do not isolate survivors to seek justice alone. A justice process that is *trauma-informed* is required, in a similar way that healthcare systems have benefited from introducing in recent years. The acknowledgement sought by survivors, and the envisioned bystander and community solidarity alongside them, might then follow this process, rather than replace it. Promising schemes of restorative justice that are innovative (and yet traditional in other cultures) are already being evaluated in some parts of the UK.

In this way, we would hope that V, and countless others with similar abusive experiences, might be more effectively freed from the constraining effects of their traumatic past, to complement our collaborative psychotherapeutic work.

Reflection point 10.1

1 Do you enquire about your clients' interactions within their virtual world? How might you incorporate this in your assessments?
2 How might we work with 'a village' (community) affected by trauma?
3 How may a systemic appreciation of your client relate to social justice?

11 Transcultural perspectives and themes on working with trauma

Divine Charura, Emma Bradshaw and Mark McFetridge

...there is an urgent need to better understand and rapidly assess for manifestations of embodied trauma, with a focus on providing a culturally informed psychological assessment method, formulation, treatment plan, and early intervention for those in distress. (O'Brien and Charura, 2022, p 1)

Culturally skilled therapists:

Understand how race, culture, ethnicity and so forth affect personality formation, *vocational choices*, manifestation of psychological disorders, help seeking behaviours *and the appropriateness or inappropriate-ness of counselling approaches*. Immigration issues, poverty, racism, stereotyping and powerlessness all leave major scars that may influence the counselling process. (Sue et al., 1992, p 482; as cited in Lago, 2010)

Overview
- This chapter will consider transcultural perspectives and themes on working with trauma.
- We consider the importance of transcultural approaches to trauma in working with those with minoritised experiences.
- We also highlight the importance of the therapeutic relationship and post-traumatic growth.
- Finally, we offer some guidance we consider helpful for transculturally informed trauma work.

Introduction

The introductory statements by Sue et al. (1992) and O'Brien and Charura (2022) at the beginning of this chapter begin to indicate the enormity, challenges and complexity of the terrain into which we need to enter, as therapists working with psychological trauma. These challenges are steeped in the paucity of culturally informed psychological assessment methods, formulations, treatment plans and provision of early interventions for those from diverse cultural backgrounds. This chapter is written as a critical chapter to go beyond the traditional perspectives which affirm the arrogance of Eurocentric modalities in being applied as a 'one size fits all' to clients and patients who present with trauma. There have been a range of strong critiques to the psychotherapy professions, which have suggested that as a Western and Eurocentric endeavour, psychotherapy is riddled with and compromised by racism (Charura & Clyburn, 2023). In this chapter we argue that, if trauma therapy is going to be fit for our contemporary culturally diverse world, and if it is to be truly demystified, then it is important that cultural conceptualisations, discrimination, racism and other 'isms' which contribute to trauma within these professions and within diverse communities are addressed head on. In relation to psychotraumatology practice and research, we also draw from Charura and Clyburn (2023, p. 72) who noted the need to 'engage critically with ideas about ontology, and, specifically, the reality that people are culturally diverse beings, and not "other" to a neutral white essence of things'. We concur that the therapeutic relationship with those presenting with trauma can only be understood in the context of trauma through the lens of relational factors, for example the fact that trauma often happens in, through or impacts relationships (Charura & Smith, 2023), and social factors, including systemic racism and oppression of those from ethnically diverse communities (Maharaj et al., 2021). Practitioners therefore must face and engage with diverse constructions and conceptualisations of psychological trauma, relational trauma, embodied trauma and presentations of mental ill health. This illuminates the importance of culture and intersectionality in understanding the experiences of individuals presenting in practice (Charura, & Smith, 2023; Grzanka et al., 2017; Maharaj et al., 2021; O'Brien & Charura, 2023).

Whilst writing this book we concurred that difficulties in developing shared and culturally sensitive understandings of trauma can hinder the therapeutic progress within our profession. Although there is increasing literature on the treatment of psychological trauma, Western conceptualisations of trauma are compromised by the limitations in existing research on transcultural perspectives of working with trauma with people from ethnically diverse and culturally diverse backgrounds. Furthermore, given that there is so much focus on PTSD and CPTSD, the cultural formulation tools from the DSM-IV, ICD-11, and *The Psychodynamic Diagnostic Manual* (PDM-2) all have limitations. We argue that while they increasingly attempt to reflect an effort to articulate diagnosis frameworks that bridge the gap between clinical complexity and empirical and methodological validity, they all remain limited. In the context of this chapter, these limitations are mainly in their engagement with the transcultural sensitivities required to equip practitioners with the depth of understanding necessary for enhancing their professional capacities to work with difference, and presentations or conceptualisations of trauma across cultures. Such capacities would inform and enhance their competencies as part of a culturally informed approach necessary for trauma work in contemporary contexts.

Refection point 11.1 – Are transcultural perspectives important in trauma work?

1 Why is it important to consider transcultural perspectives to working with trauma?
2 What challenges have you encountered, or what concerns do you have in relation to, engaging with cultural diversity in trauma work?

Why focus on a transcultural approach to trauma work and those with minoritised experiences?

In the earlier chapters of this book, we outlined some of our own reflections of the histories of trauma within our own families and generations as we have gleaned from narratives with our significant others. We concur that all trauma work in some ways is layered with cross-cultural, intergenerational and cross-systemic themes. That is, in the therapeutic relationship, there are often overlapping domains of intersectionality present between the therapist and client/s, relating to their differences and diversity in familial culture, personal cultures, age, class, etc. At the same time however, our focus in this chapter is specifically on the domain of cultural diversity with emphasis on contexts where the therapist and client not only hail from different cultures and but also where one of them is from a culturally minoritised group.

Minoritised experiences can be encapsulated by Moodley and Lubin's (2008) 'Big 7 intersectional identities,' referring to seven different facets of identity: *race (inclusive of ethnicity and culture)*, gender, class, sexual orientation, disability, age and religion (Moodley & Lubin, 2008). We draw here on Moodley's notion of those he noted as being *'outside the sentence'*. From this perspective those who are 'outside the sentence' exist in a subversive and marginal space located outside the conventional, normative epistemologies and theories that inform traditional psychological therapies (Moodley, 2009). This acknowledges the notion that therapeutic relationships are not apolitical and certainly we argue that our work with all who have experienced trauma requires us to be committed to social justice and to challenge systems of oppression and social injustice. Moodley (2009) argued that for minoritised clients, the experience of being *'outside the sentence'* produces the effect of being 'inside' another process: that of being in continual engagement with – and resistance in the face of – marginalisation, including racism, colonisation, sexism, ableism, heterosexism, ageism and classism (Moodley, 2009). Hence our focus on transcultural perspectives, in this chapter, is to ensure that our book is inclusive and that we challenge the perpetuating presentation of the deficit perspective, where focus is often on the domains of cultural difference that bring challenges to the therapeutic relationship. The chapter therefore outlines and critiques practices, approaches, and challenges and offers recommendations and considerations for practitioners engaging in trauma work from this perspective.

Current limitations that contribute to a need for more cultural awareness and sensitivity in trauma-informed care

The quote at the start of this chapter by O'Brien and Charura (2022, p. 1) highlights the need for 'culturally informed psychological assessment method, formulation, treatment plan, and early intervention for those in distress'. However, there are multiple limitations that contribute to these needs within services that provide therapeutic support for those presenting with trauma. Wylie et al. (2018) argued that paucity of transcultural awareness and care is one of the access barriers in mental health care that lead to the under-utilisation of services by those who often most need them. These, for example, include immigrants and refugees. They argued that the barriers that exist at both the individual and systemic levels include a lack of knowledge of available services and difficulties with language and communications. In the case of one of the clients we presented in Chapter 4, 'Farrokh', for example, required interpreters to translate for him in therapy and for any appointments with the hospital or home office officials.

It has also been noted that often there are cultural factors including stigma associated with mental health problems and the use of services (Wylie et al., 2018) which means that some clients and patients will not access trauma services even if they need them.

Barriers from within the health care system include limited transcultural knowledge, skills and practices among therapists. Additionally, complex trauma, such as that resulting from war, torture, displacement and resettlement, requires in-depth psychological assessments by a highly experienced, competent and culturally aware practitioner (Boyles, 2015; O'Brien & Charura, 2023). This, however, is often a limitation for many health care organisations and practitioners as therapy training does not often cover the depth required to become competent in such trauma-informed care. We have also witnessed the limitations in resources, including lack of funding for long-term therapy and systemic time constraints that undermine the ability to carry out holistic socio-culturally appropriate assessments and the offering of innovative approaches (O'Brien & Charura, 2022; O'Brien & Charura, 2023; Wylie et al., 2018).

A critical perspective: the importance of considering cultural idioms of distress and underlying systemic and historical events

We acknowledge that although trauma exposure is a global phenomenon, trauma reactions vary considerably across cultures. We agree with those who state that Western psychiatric diagnoses, such as post-traumatic stress disorder (PTSD) and complex trauma may be limited in capturing the breadth of trauma reactions in cross-cultural contexts (Patel & Hall, 2021). Furthermore, our work perspectives and critique over decades of working with individuals and families presenting with trauma in transcultural contexts, revealed for us the failures of the common diagnostic taxonomies (DSM-V, ICD-11, PDM-2). These include, for example, limitations in acknowledging the continuous stressors within the norm of experiences common to cultures with collective trauma, as well other nonphysical sources of trauma such as degradation, humiliation, oppression and the transgenerational transmission of trauma (Giladi & Bell, 2013; Kizilhan et al., 2021). Moreover, there is generally a limitation in acknowledging the centrality of religious or spiritual dimensions of conceptualising trauma, ways of healing or recovery from it and post-traumatic growth as emphasised by some people from collectivistic and faith-based cultures.

Our critique here highlights the importance of examining locally relevant reactions, such as idioms of distress and explanatory or underlying systemic or historical events that account for ongoing stress and adversity. Furthermore, we argue for culturally sensitive trauma assessment and treatment approaches, as well as a stance of practising cultural humility if as practitioners we are to be competent in working in culturally diverse contexts (Kirmayer et al., 2014; Patel & Hall, 2021; Pedersen et al., 2010; Sinalo, 2019).

In our review of literature, we position our critiques within the context of global mental health, humanitarian and postcolonial, transcultural psychotraumatology. We have noted critical perspectives which we agreed would enable us as practitioners to enhance our knowledge and capacity to work in transcultural contexts. With regard to consideration of how within a transculturally informed perspective it is important to view trauma, beyond seeing it as exposure to a particular event, but considering historical and current contexts, we draw on some international bodies of work (Benda & Pells, 2020; Kirmayer et al., 2014; Pedersen et al., 2010; Pells et al., 2022; Summerfield, 2022). Pedersen et al. (2010) for example reported how the highland Quechua people of northern Ayacucho construct and experience expressions of distress and suffering such as 'pinsamientuwan' (worrying thoughts, worries), 'ñakary' (suffering) and llaki (sorrow, sadness), in a context of persistent social inequalities, social exclusion and a recent history of political violence.

Antic (2022) highlighted how working with some individuals presenting with trauma included understanding their cultural frame of reference in which their conceptualisation of trauma included belief in vengeful spirits or displeased ancestors, thereby reflecting cultural practices carrying externalised attributions for adversity. Practitioners are invited and challenged to engage with wider perspectives of trauma. These should for example include going beyond seeing it as exposure to particular violent or horrifying events, but to also consider for example a life of hunger, poverty and lack of any viable opportunities (Antic, 2022; Summerfield, 2022).

On the one hand we acknowledge that PTSD is often typically conceptualised as a discrete extreme event (APA, 2013). However, on the other hand, on reflecting on global historical and current events, we have noted the impact of war and multiple historic genocides and current atrocities as well as conflicts on different continents. To consider the elongated impact of the conflict context, for example, it is estimated that 5 million children under the age of 5 died as a result of armed conflict in Africa in 1995 to 2015 (Wagner et al., 2018). What place do these children and their families have in public consciousness, and how can a trauma diagnostic taxonomy capture this generational trauma?

As psychologists who are interested in trauma work, we have all been engaged in dialogue about humanity and the underlying causes of genocide (Wagner et al, 2018). Two of us have independently visited Cambodia (DC and MM) and were moved to learn of the genocide that took place there which resulted in the deaths of 1.5 to 2 million people from 1975 to 1979, nearly a quarter of Cambodia's population in 1975. We have reflected on the trauma and transgenerational trauma that many people still continued to experience, voice and reflect on. We draw on the work of Sinalo (2019), who noted how the perspective of trauma in relation to genocide does not often account for the roots of genocide in colonial divisionism and post-independence authoritarianism. Although her work was focusing on the genocide that occurred in Rwanda, we agree that her assertions apply to other genocide contexts and that this often results in the application of a trauma paradigm that is frequently dehistoricised and decontextualised (Benda & Pells, 2020; Pells et al., 2022; Sinalo, 2019). Thus, rather than viewing genocide as a single event giving rise to trauma, Sinalo (2019: 31) argues that genocide can be viewed as 'a much more complex, chronic form of trauma' which encompasses the structural violence of colonialism, neo-colonialism, and authoritarianism, and with enduring legacies in the present. Pells et al. (2022), highlighted that this perspective calls for practitioners to engage with the realities of 'colonial legacies and their interconnection to social trauma', and the dislocation of social and cultural institutions as well as the resulting ongoing direct and structural forms of violence.

Our critique here therefore invites practitioners to engage with the theorisation on trauma and traumatic legacies, in ways that adopt more expansive understandings of both distress and healing beyond a focus on the individual and the event. It is important to recognise and address external, ongoing sources of distress, trauma and how these are rooted in historical and current systemic oppressions, including intergenerational trauma (Hinton and Lewis-Fernández, 2011; Kirmayer et al., 2014). Accordingly, we assert that from a transcultural perspective, it is important to understand and consider multiple expressions of psychological and trauma distress as closely related to past and current events, shaped by beliefs, core values and cultural norms. Through this process, our understanding of trauma and the interventions we offer can be transformed and recreated and we can then invest in new meanings and a paradigm shift on how we can work effectively with trauma and complex trauma work (Pedersen et al., 2010). The section that follows outlines some perspectives on intergenerational trauma through the lens of epigenetics.

Transgenerational transmission of trauma and transcultural perspectives

Having briefly introduced transgenerational trauma and epigenetics in Chapter 3, we are aware that the transgenerational transmission of trauma is a controversial issue which has been explored in over five hundred articles, and these have reported mixed findings of this phenomenon (Braga et al., 2012; Kirmayer et al., 2014; Kizilhan et al., 2021; Lago & Charura, 2015). Our intention in this section of this chapter is not to review the literature on transgenerational trauma but to outline the importance of practitioners working with trauma to be mindful of such perspectives which particularly clients of a different cultural root to the main Western culture here, may be familiar with. We also briefly outline some ways that may be helpful in working with clients who present with transgenerational trauma.

We draw from a study on mice by Dias & Ressler (2014) published in *Nature Neuroscience*, in which they wafted acetophenone scent (a chemical with a scent compared to that of cherries and almonds) around a small chamber, while giving small electric shocks to male mice. They noted that over time, these mice eventually learned to associate the acetophenone scent with pain, shuddering in the presence of the acetophenone scent even without a shock. The researchers then bred the mice and surprisingly despite never having encountered acetophenone in their lives, the offspring exhibited increased sensitivity when introduced to the acetophenone scent, shuddering more markedly. This observation was also noted in the third generation of mice (their 'grandchildren') (Dias & Ressler, 2014). Mice conceived through *in vitro* fertilisation with sperm from males sensitised to acetophenone also reacted the same. It was also noted that similar experiments showed that the response can also be transmitted down from the mother.

Similar to Lago and Charura's (2014) reflections, we too are aware of the limitations and biases that this study may raise, such as the issues of animal welfare and the lack of generalisability to humans. However, we value its contribution to our understanding of how a traumatic experience and stressful environmental factors can influence biology through 'epigenetic' modifications, which alter the expression of genes, but not their actual nucleotide sequence (Dias & Ressler, 2014). Pérez Alvarez highlighted that humans can also inherit epigenetic alterations/modifications that influence their behaviour and argued that there are possibilities of predisposition/susceptibility to psychological distress relating to trauma through this (González-Pardo & Pérez Álvarez, 2013; Lago & Charura, 2015).

Additionally, it would also be important to consider epigenetic factors such as life adversities (trauma, disorganised attachment, etc.) as related to its clinical manifestations, rather than genetic factors. While it is also accepted that behaviour and environment will finally take on a leading role in human development through epigenetic mechanisms (González-Pardo & Pérez Álvarez, 2013), our interest in epigenetics and such studies (Braga et al., 2012; Dias & Ressler, 2014; Gapp et al., 2014; Kirmayer et al., 2014; Kizilhan et al., 2021) enhances our thinking on the implications of epigenetics, environment, culture and the possibilities of transgenerational trauma. In addition, through our therapeutic work we have consistently come across clients whose cultural and religious belief systems encompass an understanding of transgenerational trauma, and its manifestation, in clients' different cultures. These ways for example include descriptions that include 'soul wound' which relates to how trauma impacts on the lives of many people who are members of a cultural group that are subjected to various forms of violence, injustice and oppression (Duran, 2006). Vontress and Epp (1997) noted the term 'historical hostility' to describe a pattern of responses that many African-Americans exhibit, which they argued may stem from their prolonged subjection to inferior treatment in American society (Vontress & Epp, 1997). They also noted the term 'transgenerational hatred', to refer to how the hatred of specific others or specific groups is maintained over long periods of time and across generations.

Hall (2009) in his writing on the transgenerational trauma arising from enslavement used the term 'existential crucifixion' to describe the impact of the horrific struggles of enslaved Africans and how their lives were decimated through slavery (Hall, 2009). Transgenerational trauma has also been referred to as *'continuous trauma'* to describe the experience of being within a continuous disempowered minority position, following the context of Straker and the Sanctuaries team in their work with South African youth during the anti-apartheid struggle where people experienced ongoing fears of detention, torture and death (Straker, 1987, 1990). Alleyne, (2004) made reference to the terms *'identity wounding'*, *'internal oppressor'* and *'internalized oppression'* and reflected on the traumatic impact of being discriminated against for who you are, as well as the impact of 'prejudices, projections, inter-generational wounds.' Furthermore, she highlighted the impact of one's historical past, the dynamic of developing an inner tyrant which she termed 'the internal oppressor' and consequently the process of absorbing the values and beliefs of the oppressor. She noted that through this process clients who present, for example, with racial trauma would often have come to believe that the stereotypes and misinformation about their group is true (or partly true) (Alleyne, 2004, 2011). We also note here that other concepts include 'racism as trauma' (Bains, 2010), (please also see writing on working with racial trauma; Charura & Al-Murri 2024) and 'recognition trauma' (McKenzie-Mavinga, 2009).

While we cannot go into the diversity of terms here that people from different cultures use to describe experiences or their awareness of transgenerational impacts of trauma, we hope to raise awareness in you, the reader, of this.

Following on from the studies we reviewed, and from our clinical experience of working in multicultural contexts, we have noted different ways of working with transgenerational trauma including employing therapeutic techniques that address the neurobiology of trauma. These include, for example, interventions that reduce the activation of the amygdala and hypothalamus while simultaneously increasing activity of the frontal lobe (i.e. eye movement desensitisation and reprocessing – EMDR) and a diversity of culturally tailored modalities and therapeutic techniques which stimulate focusing on challenging negative thoughts associated with the trauma (Lago & Charura, 2015). Working with the client's narrative and paying detail to the unspoken trauma in the client's family enables the problems and traumatic experiences such as displacement, torture, violence and so on to be re-told (Beaudoin, 2005). The role of therapy is to unpack the cultural conceptualisation of the trauma narrative and its cultural underpinnings, to explore the shift in the individual's concept of self as a result of the experience. Furthermore, it is to make visible information or perspectives that would have been neglected through the silencing of the trauma narrative (Beaudoin, 2022; Lago & Charura, 2015; Lago & Hirai, 2013; Smale & Perry, 2003). Other perspectives have noted the importance of working with metaphors and stories in talking about transgenerational traumas as clients may find it easier to confront painful experiences in this way (Lago & Charura, 2015; Smale & Perry, 2003).

Connolly, in her paper 'Healing the wounds of our fathers' (2011), noted three fundamental aspects that she stated are transmitted inter-generationally and she identified these as 'death of time', which refers to the discontinuity between past, present and future that survivors of collective trauma experienced and transmitted to their children: 'death of language' which refers to how trauma can result in loss of language. In relation to this it is also noted that the 'death of language' also profoundly modifies the capacity to create dream metaphors and to link them together to create narratives (Connolly, 2011). We are also reminded of research which described trauma as a speechless horror due to the suppression of Broca's area of the brain during trauma experiences (van der Kolk, 2014). Additionally, Connolly (2011) describes death of narrative as present in intergenerational manifestations of trauma too, and she stated, 'creating meaningful narratives about the experience of extreme trauma is a difficult and painful task whether this has been experienced or transmitted' (p. 614). Connolly suggests that in working with clients in the therapeutic relationship, practitioners need to ensure that they pay attention to these aspects by allowing for the untold death of time, death of language and death of narrative to be told.

Post-traumatic growth and the therapeutic relationship

There has been increasing literature and research also into the cross-cultural variations of client resilience, post-traumatic growth and subsequent perceptions of how people develop following experiences of trauma (Taylor et al., 2020). Others have queried the manifestation of the 'post' in *'post-traumatic-growth'* arguing that this is not always applicable as stressors for many individuals, families and communities are ongoing (Ali et al., 2023). While we covered some research in earlier chapters and there is more on post-traumatic growth in our final chapter, in this chapter we want to highlight that practitioners need to be aware of their assumptions and perceptions of post-traumatic growth as well as the limitations of therapy with different clients. We draw here on the work of Diamond et al. (2013) who referred to this as 'ongoing traumatic stress response' (OTSR). They stated that OTSR is not a diagnosis nor label, but an alternative framework through which to make sense of intense psychological suffering in situations where people face ongoing traumatic stress (Diamond et al., 2013).

We also acknowledge and value that many of the clients we work with, including the clients we present as part of our case studies, are engaged in long-term psychotherapy for trauma, over many years, to recover from their distress. Farrokh, for example, through what he described as healing, established a new relationship.

With particular reference to what we see as the developmental needs for transcultural skills that the therapist requires to be competent in when working in transcultural contexts, we note that our task is to co-create a 'good-enough', culturally sensitive and authentic relationship with the client that fosters therapeutic capability. We have noted the following as helpful:

Box 11.1 Helpful reflections for transculturally informed trauma work

Developmental needs for transcultural skills

1 Be continually vigilant as a therapist to what your perceptions, projections and behaviours are towards a client whom you conceive to be different or diverse.

2 Hold in mind and in supervision that no client is reducible to a set of identities, label, i.e. PTSD, or to a set of cultural expectations, a set of theoretical postulates, or a range of assumptions, hailing from our own cultural bias.

3 It is important to understand culturally (including religious/faith/spirituality) differing notions that apply to clients you work with of trauma, distress, disease, and 'wellness'. (What does it mean to be experiencing trauma, or what does it mean to be well?)

4 As a therapist it is important to be aware of your own 'otherness', your various identities, and the projections that the client may have towards you. It is key to understand the historical, structural and social traumas, including racism, the legacy of slavery, the holocaust, genocides, poverty etc.)

5 It is important to have access to and be prepared to employ 'culturally relevant' assessment and formulation tools, interventions and referral resources.

6 Be aware of your own personal and professional qualities; possess the appropriate knowledge and professional competencies for engaging in transcultural trauma work with clients from ethnically diverse communities.

7 Have the professional commitment to continually develop yourself, as well as your knowledge of different contexts and cultures, and to engage in culturally appropriate assessments and interventions.

8 Engage in supervision that is culturally sensitive and open to challenging the cultural bias of one's approach and anti-oppressive practice in relation to the trauma work and holding positions of not knowing and holding power with clients rather than over clients.

9 Be prepared and be open to authentically engage with bodies of knowledge and cultures which value altered states of consciousness, spiritual formulations of trauma, perspectives on collective or transgenerational trauma, somatic and traditional healing therapeutic approaches or ways of treatment. Be open to working with dreams and other culturally relevant areas for the clients you will be working with.

10 Be committed to social justice and decolonised approaches which are inclusive and affirming of human agency and capacity for working collaboratively with others to challenge all forms of 'isms' and to create change.

(Please see: Charura & Lago, 2021a; Charura & Lago, 2021b; Lago, 2006; Lago, 2010; Lago, 2011; Paul & Charura, 2014; Sweeney et al., 2021; Winter & Charura, 2023)

Reflection point 11.2 – Reflecting on personal and professional development

1 Reflect on your practice, and on the recommendations noted here. What do you see as missing from your own practice?

2 What will you develop and how will you achieve this to become more culturally competent in working with clients from ethnically diverse communities?

Conclusion

In concluding this chapter, we assert that the benefit of a transculturally informed therapeutic approach to trauma enables continued development of understanding of how mental health and experiences of trauma are informed by cultural values. Consequences of cultural misunderstandings and dismissal of clients' cultural belief systems and norms can be significant, as this can lead to incomplete assessments, incorrect diagnoses, inadequate or inappropriate treatment, and failed treatment alliances. These problems in the least can be costly, both in terms of increased service use and in terms of poor clinical outcomes (Wylie et al., 2018) and at worst we argue could be unethical. In line with this we appreciate Sweeney et al.'s (2021), formulated evidence-based guidelines for conducting trauma-informed talking therapy assessments which highlight the importance of understanding the historical, structural and social traumas, including racism and discrimination (Sweeney et al., 2021). We have therefore made a case in this chapter for adopting more expansive understandings of both psychological distress, trauma/complex trauma, and healing beyond a focus on the individual and the event. It is important to recognise and address external, ongoing sources of distress and trauma and how these are rooted in historical and current systemic oppressions. We must engage with decolonising approaches and demonstrate an awareness as well as commitment to social justice, and its intricate links to the personal, to society, diverse communities and to our professions. Furthermore, we must respond in and out of the therapy room in ways that demonstrate that we value the views and lived experiences of others. This illuminates the contemporary shift of a social justice informed approach of 'power-with' rather than 'power-over' – the voice of the client and a shift from the position of expert to that of having cultural humility and truly valuing diversity.

12 Trauma demystified... the next steps

Emma Bradshaw, Divine Charura and Mark McFetridge

Overview

- This chapter will present a summary of what the book has covered so far.
- The concept of post-traumatic growth will be discussed at both an individual and societal level.
- Post-traumatic growth will be considered in relation to the case studies of Little V, Farrokh and Willow.
- Possible future directions in relation to the next steps in understanding trauma will be proposed.
- To conclude, a summary of the key themes of this book will be given.

Introduction

We started this book by introducing how we would navigate the contemporary and contentious perspectives surrounding psychological trauma in current times. The perspectives we have considered have included a combination of biological, psychological, social, sexual, spiritual and cultural aspects to ensure a thorough overview of trauma is given. Throughout the book, we have aimed to stimulate thought, challenge assumptions and to illuminate traumatic responses from an alternative perspective.

In the second chapter, we considered the historical context of trauma, examining how preceding centuries have shaped present-day narratives, highlighting the complexity of trauma from diverse viewpoints. Our exploration defined trauma and scrutinised its interpretation through varying lenses. We drew upon transgenerational narratives and considered the perspectives of trauma from the authors' personal experiences.

Chapter 3 aimed to go beyond the presentation and nature of trauma as being intrapsychic. We focused on the formulation of trauma from a perspective which included biological, psychological, social, cultural and spiritual factors which we proposed is key to our relational understanding of trauma. We illustrated this in Chapter 4 by introducing our case examples of Farrokh, Little V and Willow, to demonstrate how our theoretical understanding might manifest in practice. We continued to use these fictional cases throughout the book to further illustrate the points we make.

In Chapter 5, we provided a critique of current research in the trauma field. We made a case for, and provided examples of, creative, critical and transcultural methodologies within trauma research. We then, in Chapter 6, introduced and critiqued the concept of psychopathology, with reference to diagnostic tools. We considered the origins of the term 'complex trauma' with reference to a relational, trauma-informed perspective.

Chapter 7 addressed contemporary trauma approaches and their limitations, considering the value and limitations in healthcare delivery which is led by NICE guideline recommended therapies. We explored the position of evidence-based therapies and considered future possibilities of trauma therapies.

The role of moral trauma was acknowledged in Chapter 8, highlighting the experiences of key workers during the Covid-19 pandemic. In addition, case examples addressed the issue of interconnectedness with traumatic memory, questioning the assumption of accuracy and the implications of such.

Importantly, in Chapter 9 we recognised the fundamental role that love and relationships play in the trauma landscape. We emphasised the pivotal role of the therapeutic relationship when working with those who have experienced trauma. We also acknowledged the importance of clinical supervision and raised awareness of the possibility of vicarious trauma.

Contemporary systemic perspectives were explored in Chapter 10, including working with couples and families. We highlighted a relational understanding of the impact of trauma on the family system and emphasised the importance of considering the uniqueness of each context when formulating the individual's traumatic experience.

Our penultimate chapter contemplated a range of cross-cultural approaches to working with trauma, from both Eurocentric and non-Eurocentric perspectives. Examples were given of trauma work in cross-cultural contexts with diverse communities who conceptualise trauma differently from that classically noted in Eurocentric texts.

In this concluding chapter, our focus shifts to the concept of post-traumatic growth arising from the aftermath of trauma. We introduce and dissect the meaning of post-traumatic growth, adopting a critical standpoint consistent with the overarching bio-psycho-social-sexual-spiritual-cultural lens. Applying this concept to the cases of Farrokh, Little V and Willow, we provide an illustration of what post-traumatic growth might entail for our clients.

Looking ahead, we briefly outline considerations and possibilities for the future evolution of our knowledge and practices in the field of trauma. Then, in conclusion, we summarise the key themes of the book, leaving you with valuable insights to apply in your clinical practice, hoping these messages resonate as you navigate the complexities of trauma.

Trauma and post-traumatic growth at an individual level

The experience of trauma can affect the very core of a person's being. It can impact the beliefs that a person has about themselves as well as influencing the way they see the world. It is therefore inevitable that the person's path in life changes, and the process of moving forward, or growing, will be impacted. It has been observed that people who have experienced adversity, trauma or highly challenging life circumstances, may not simply return to how things were before, but may experience personal growth by reconfiguring their understanding of the world in a way that incorporates the trauma, so that their experience of life is more enhanced than it was before. While this concept itself is not new, these changes in a traumatised person have been studied in the field of positive psychology, with the term 'post-traumatic growth' being first used by psychologists Richard Tedeschi and Lawrence Calhoun in the 1990s to refer to the positive aspect of psychological change that can take place after an adverse life event (Tedeschi & Calhoun, 2004)

Since then, the phenomenon of post-traumatic growth has been widely studied and there is now a plethora of literature focusing on this concept. However, the complexities of this field are widespread and are highlighted by Jayawickreme and Blackie (2014) who observe that in the research literature, not only is there a lack of agreement on what term is used to describe the phenomenon, but the related theories each have a slightly different focus, making them difficult to compare. To illustrate their point, they refer to four theories which conceptualise post-traumatic growth: one which focuses on eudaimonic (psychological) wellbeing (Joseph & Linley, 2005, 2008); a model of post-traumatic growth which focuses on the change in an individual's life narrative (Pals, 2006); an 'action-focused growth' theory which focuses on the behavioural change that follows the experience of trauma (Hobfoll et al., 2007); and the dominant model which sees post-traumatic growth as both a process and an outcome (Tedeschi & Calhoun, 2004).

To understand the phenomenon of post-traumatic growth in greater depth, a 21-item scale called the Post-Traumatic Growth Inventory (PTGI) was introduced (Tedeschi & Calhoun, 1996) to quantify the growth that can arise from individuals navigating and coping with traumatic events. The inventory suggests five potential areas of growth, namely: appreciation of life; relationships with others; recognition of new possibilities in life; heightened feelings of personal strength; and a greater engagement with spirituality. This indicates that post-traumatic growth can encompass a confluence of biological, psychological, social, sexual, spiritual and cultural factors.

Aside from the acknowledgement that models of post-traumatic growth have a different focus, it has also been noted that the scientific methods used to study post-traumatic growth are flawed because individuals are asked about their growth but are not given the opportunity to report on the negative impact of their trauma. This has led to consideration of how future research into this area can be conducted, with Jayawickreme and Blackie (2014) suggesting that exploring post-traumatic growth in relation to the study of personality will establish whether changes following trauma reflect actual change or are instead a presentation of pre-existing resilience.

In addition to the aspects of post-traumatic growth mentioned above, another stance is a biological one. We discussed in Chapter 3 how the experience of trauma can biologically induce changes in the nervous system and physical health. Likewise, it has been found that post-traumatic growth can correlate with physiological changes too. These findings were examined in a systematic review and meta-analysis which explored the impact of three types of psychological therapy (cognitive processing therapy (CPT); eye movement desensitisation and reprocessing (EMDR) and prolonged exposure (PE) therapy) on neural activity underlying the phenomenon of post-traumatic growth for adult trauma survivors. With the aim of assessing the relationship between brain function and post-traumatic growth (measured by the PTGI before and after therapy), Pierce et al. (2023) concluded that therapy, particularly EMDR therapy, has a robust impact on post-traumatic growth and brain function. One example given is that EMDR has been found to activate the thalamus which increases the capacity to regulate the autonomic nervous system, thereby reducing the physiological symptoms of PTSD, clearly helpful in relation to post-traumatic growth.

In Chapter 3 we also considered how the experience of trauma can understandably have a significant psychological impact: instigating distressing emotions, disturbing cognitions and challenges to the way that a person understands the world and their place in it. The concept of post-traumatic growth would indicate that an individual finds a way to live with and/or change these psychological experiences. After experiencing trauma, a person might find that their hopes, dreams and assumptions about life are shattered. The concept of growth comes from not simply having experienced a trauma, but from the way in which an individual reconfigures their life afterwards.

As mentioned above, our capacity to do this may link to our personality, in that the ability to experience post-traumatic growth may be influenced by the personality type of an individual, with those who are more extravert, open to change – as measured by the NEO Personality Inventory (Costa & McCrae, 1992) – and those who are optimistic, having a greater propensity to psychologically grow from their experience (Tedeschi and Calhoun, 2004). It has been more recently proposed that post-traumatic growth can be viewed in terms of positive personality change, where changes in patterns of thoughts, feelings and behaviours lead individuals to respond in a particular way after the experience of trauma. While this perspective is partly to address methodological difficulties, it also provides an alternative way of looking at the processes which underlie post-traumatic growth (Jayawickreme et al., 2021).

Post-traumatic growth frequently manifests as a psychological coping mechanism, where individuals seek to navigate and rebuild their lives in the aftermath of a traumatic event. It is not necessarily a purposeful or conscious pursuit of a better life but rather a natural response to the challenges posed by the trauma. Significantly, Tedeschi and Calhoun (2004) highlight that the occurrence of post-traumatic growth does not necessarily correlate with reduced psychological distress. They emphasise that post-traumatic growth often coexists with the enduring pain of the trauma, rather than serving as a replacement.

Individuals who are on the path to recovery or healing from trauma often seize the opportunity to align with their core values, a pivotal process that significantly shapes the choices governing their lifestyles. This transformative journey may involve prioritising certain aspects of their lives while re-evaluating others. Notably, as individuals begin to recover, they may experience a heightened autonomy in decision-making, becoming less swayed by external influences and more attuned to their personal priorities.

Another important aspect of post-traumatic growth is the spiritual impact on an individual, with some people seeing coping with trauma as part of the path of their spiritual journey. Spirituality can be a moderator of distress, linking to the popular belief that coping with adversity can make you stronger. The spiritual aspect of post-traumatic growth has been observed in many contexts including the scientific study of near-death experiences (NDE). In Chapter 6 we saw how the DSM-5 recognises that a factor which can lead to the development of PTSD is when an individual feels that their life has been threatened. Conversely, for some, an NDE can lead to a spiritual experience which is viewed as positive. This was first brought to the fore in the 1970s by doctor and researcher Raymond Moody in his seminal book *Life After Life* (Moody, 2001). Moody spoke to patients who had survived resuscitation following cardiac arrest. A number of those who had clinically died but had come back to life were able to report their experience of death. Themes of transcendence and a glimpse into a realm beyond the physical were recalled with mentions of a bright light, a feeling of peace and a sense of connection to something greater: all commonly associated with spiritual experiences. Since then, a great deal of further research has been conducted in this area. In one review of studies exploring near death experiences, Parnia et al. (2007) found that 'in general, those who have had a NDE are happier, more socially orientated, less materialistic, more altruistic and less afraid of death than those who do not have this experience'.

Post-traumatic growth at a societal level

At a societal level, we have acknowledged how the experience of trauma can impact relationships, with those who have experienced trauma finding it difficult to trust or preferring to stay within their 'comfort zone'. Likewise, post-traumatic growth can also occur within the context of relationships and interpersonal connections. Growth after trauma can be a transformative journey which may include an enhanced appreciation for relationships and an improved capacity to connect with and support others.

It has even been found that some of those who experience post-traumatic growth are able to relate better than before: for example, rape victims may make decisions in their relationships which prevent them from experiencing further abuse (Tedeschi & Calhoun, 1996). Those who have experienced the loss of someone they love may find that their other relationships become deeper and even more important to them than they were before the loss (Calhoun et al., 2000) which ties in with the concept of love, that we have already talked about in Chapter 9.

At a wider level, several cross-cultural issues have been raised in response to the current research on post-traumatic growth. These have been highlighted by Kashyap and Hussain (2018) who cite studies which promote the importance of cultural awareness in this field (see Key resources and further reading on page 131).

The key points they raise include the observation that much of the current research on post-traumatic growth has been conducted from an etic (outside) perspective which is not applicable across all cultures. Therefore, while some cultures may think of an event as traumatic, others might view it differently within their own cultural framework. The alternative of adopting an emic (internal) approach could shift the perspective to be more culturally inclusive.

Another point is the difference between proximate and distal influences. The former may include family, friends, social and religious groups, while the latter relates to wider societal influences. The impact of each may depend on whether the individual lives in an individualist or collectivist society.

There may also be cultural differences on rumination, cognitive strategies and growth. Culture may influence the level of personal responsibility felt, with those from collectivist cultures considering the effect of the trauma on others as well as themselves.

It is suggested that the theories of post-traumatic growth may also have a cultural bias. The proposal that trauma challenges an individual's assumptive world, leading to emotional distress and subsequent growth (Tedeschi & Calhoun, 1996), may lack cultural specificity as those from individualist cultures may prioritise personal experiences and change, whereas those from a collectivist culture may focus more on social roles (Kashyap & Hussain, 2018).

A final issue relates to the measurement of post-traumatic growth. It is proposed that the cultural validity of quantitative measures can present challenges. An alternative methodology to consider is qualitative research methods, such as semi-structured interviews, which can provide more culturally sensitive insights and may enhance the transcultural assessment of post-traumatic growth (Kashyap & Hussain, 2018).

We therefore emphasise that the notion of post-traumatic growth demands careful consideration, and the experience of each individual person will be different. Unrealistic expectations, both from individuals and society, that those who have endured trauma must not only recover but emerge from the experience in an enhanced state can prove detrimental. This point was emphasised in a study of women who experienced birth trauma (Beck & Watson, 2016), where recommendation was given to clinicians to walk alongside those they are helping: respecting the adversity they have experienced and holding the possibility of post-traumatic growth in mind, without it becoming an expectation which may inadvertently contribute to feelings of inadequacy.

In addition, as therapists we recognise the importance of adopting a critical approach to thinking about trauma, not only to facilitate understanding of the concept of trauma but also to inform our ability to help our clients. When considering post-traumatic growth, it is important to reflect on our own position, and whether we are avoiding the painful reality of how difficult it is for someone as we help them to work through the worst moments of their life. We need to ensure that we are not focusing on post-traumatic growth as an avoidance of a harsh reality which, as therapists, we find very difficult to engage with.

This point was emphasised by a lead researcher of dialectical behavioural therapy (DBT), Melanie Harned (2022) who realised that DBT therapists were reluctant to do the trauma-processing phase of the work after their clients were stabilised. She expressed concern that, as this is such difficult therapeutic work, the focus was on coping skills and therapists were avoiding addressing the effects of trauma that were being experienced by clients. It is therefore important to consider whether we can be supported to contain the work that we are doing. If not, we may be in danger of turning away from it and focusing on post-traumatic growth instead, to avoid the pain of working through just how terrible it was for the individual, thereby denying them the opportunity of working towards their own healing point.

To conclude our thoughts about post-traumatic growth, we would first like to clearly acknowledge our belief that experiencing trauma should not simply be viewed as a stepping stone to post-traumatic growth. Traumatic events can be horrific for individuals and those around them, and we have no wish to minimise the deep pain that can be experienced. While it is possible for people to find growth after trauma, this does not mean that they are glad that the traumatic event happened (Tedeschi & Calhoun, 2004). We therefore need to think about what happens to the 'core wounding'. For many of those we have worked with, trauma goes well beyond the first stage of coping with the initial distress. In terms of physical trauma, for example, if your hand was severed by a machete (thinking of some people DC has spoken to from Rwanda) there will be a massive scar. Maybe that hand will never be as strong as it once was. So, with physical trauma we can come to accept our limitations. Likewise, for psychological trauma, a person may accept that they will not have the same strength as they did before but may find a new path forward that can be rewarding to them in a different way. The traumatic grief or loss which is experienced may never end…so perhaps instead, the concept of a post-traumatic life is what can be considered.

Case Studies

Little V

Considering the case of Little V, with help and time she started to recover psychologically from the trauma that she experienced; however, her body was badly mutilated with self-harm scars. When she had managed not to self-harm for two years, the surgeons said that she could have the option of plastic surgery to repair her wounds. Little V decided not to have the surgery because she didn't want to hide her scars as seeing the scars gave her strength: these were the scars of what she had been through and moved on from, so to remove the scars which meant something to her would have felt like a weakness to her.

Farrokh

We can also think about the post-traumatic life for Farrokh, who had been tortured. In some of the therapy sessions he had spoken about and also shown some of his scars. He even alluded to scars on his genitalia and had spoken about the horrible things that had happened in the torture chambers. He had worked through the trauma therapy for a few years with me (DC) and the interpreter (whose role is important to acknowledge).

Before ending the therapy, he had said to me that he did not think that talking about it had done much good. I questioned the effectiveness of therapy and therefore thought that my three-week holiday would be inconsequential. However, on my return Farrokh was angry with me for having been away and abandoning him. At that point I was reminded of the power of relationship. We continued to work together for another year on a weekly basis and he never missed a session. For much of the time, the interpreter and I were the only people he would see.

Eventually, therapy ended as planned, and Farrokh got status in the UK as a refugee seeking sanctuary. I met him a few years ago at a food festival and he was with a beautiful young woman who he introduced to me as his wife (he had been married before but had lost contact through what had happened). Farrokh also had a beautiful daughter and was very pleased to introduce his family to me. For one of the few times in all the time I've known him, he smiled. I expressed how lovely it was to meet him and his beautiful family. I will never know if Farrokh experienced post-traumatic joy or growth but certainly something had shifted, and I would like to think that the work we had done with trauma and other social networks had helped him to get to this point in his post-traumatic life.

Willow

The process of being diagnosed with autism facilitated a shift for Willow. She was entitled to more support in school, and this continued as she went to university: the first member of her family to do so. Willow worked with a therapist for two years, which helped her to understand and process her experience of trauma in the context of being autistic. Willow's relationship with her family is still difficult but has become easier now that she no longer lives at home. Willow gradually began a process of self-acceptance which is still ongoing and is helping her to move forward with her life. She realised that being autistic is not something that she can change and will continue to be challenging at times throughout her life; however through therapy she came to realise that how she responds to her own needs as an autistic person is something that she can change. Willow has learnt that when she feels over-whelmed in a noisy environment, she can retreat to her room in the university accommodation and have some quiet time. When she feels overwhelmed, she may need to take some time out to pace herself. She accepts that she finds it difficult to socialise in big groups of people, but she does have a couple of individual friends that she gets on well with and is happy with that.

Future directions: the next steps in understanding trauma

Throughout this book we have reviewed the developments in the field of psy-chological trauma and given an overview of current dialogues, acknowledging that how we understand and manage trauma has changed over time. Of course, our knowledge of how trauma impacts those affected is dynamic: it is constantly evolving and will continue to change going forwards. Furthermore, self-reflection is essential to identify the impact that the work has on us as therapists and to address and manage any vicarious trauma that we may experience. Personal therapy, supervision, peer support and other continuing professional and per-sonal development activities may be ways to ensure self-care.

The future directions of trauma are multi-faceted, with change affecting aspects such as the nature of the traumatic events themselves, our knowledge and understanding of how trauma impacts us, as well as the continuous evolu-tion of treatment modalities which are offered to those who are suffering.

While many categories of traumatic events are historic and will sadly con-tinue to affect individuals and society in the future, some traumatic incidents are unprecedented and warrant research to inform relevant action and policy making. At a societal level we often notice a shift in thinking due to shock fac-tor. When there is a new type of event in life that shocks us, or takes us by surprise, our previous sense of security is shaken. One such example is the emerging evidence that offenders are using immersive technology to abuse children (Allen & McIntosh, 2023). As we have not had previous understanding of this type of abuse, we are unable to fully understand what the impact will be going forwards, leaving us in anticipation of the consequences that may only reveal themselves over time.

Another example is the prevalence of trauma in lesbian, gay, bisexual, trans-gender and queer (LGBTQ) individuals. These individuals not only experience higher rates of discrimination, victimisation and minority stress, but do not always have a positive experience in healthcare and often have to contend with ongoing minority stress after PTSD has been treated (Livingston et al., 2020).

Simultaneously, the landscape of treatment modalities is impacted by new advances. One example is the use of virtual reality (VR) to aid trauma therapy

(Katz et al., 2020). Another is the renewed interest in the use of psychedelic drugs to enhance trauma recovery. While psychedelic drugs have been used historically across diverse cultures to heal trauma (George et al., 2020), contemporary studies have been exploring the benefits of their controlled therapeutic application in the Western world, with trauma treatment clinics starting to offer these interventions (Krediet et al., 2020).

Further to this, one point of note is the consideration of whether future directions are reconfigurations of what has already been studied in the past. This point was observed by Judith Herman in her book *Trauma and Recovery* (Herman, 1992/2022) where she noted how past advances in trauma treatment have been researched and then forgotten, before being taken up again at a later point in time.

To illustrate this point, DC recalls a trip to India, accompanied by two students. On an encounter with a Buddhist community, one of the students commented to a monk how much she likes mindfulness. The monk responded 'Well, of course in India we've been practising Buddhism here for over 1000 years, not just mindfulness as you're calling it now'. The point of what he said really resonated: he was referring to the commercialisation of mindfulness. It could be argued that a similar point could be made about the commodification of trauma treatment. We do, of course, acknowledge the positive point that there is an increased awareness of trauma. People in all areas of society are beginning to understand what trauma is and are encouraged to provide 'trauma-informed' care. However, one concern is how trauma care has become a commodity: you can get treatment for it, or have therapy for it, and this will cost you a certain amount.

We conclude by emphasising that while many contemporary interventions demonstrate efficacy, it is important to hold a balanced perspective: drawing on the wisdom of the past while embracing the innovations of the future. To transcend the commercialisation of healing, it is imperative not to lose sight of the enduring importance of returning to the 'I-thou' relationship which encompasses love and connection.

Key themes of this book

Having considered post-traumatic living, linked this to our case studies and considered the potential work in the field of trauma going forwards, our final task is to describe the key themes that we have highlighted throughout this book to summarise the main points that we have made.

1. A multi-dimensional view

First and foremost, trauma can significantly impact us in different domains across cultures and difference. The impact of trauma impacts us biologically, psychologically, socially, sexually, spiritually and existentially. Clinicians working with traumatised individuals will benefit from holding these perspectives in mind when working with their clients and maintaining a curious stance as to the experience of the individual person in their unique circumstances.

2. The context of relationship

Given that we are relational beings, trauma often happens in the context of relationship or is associated with relationships and therefore we assert that working through trauma is also likely to occur in relationship and in this book, we are proposing, through a therapeutic relationship.

3. Ethical considerations

The third point we would like to make is about ethics and the concept of doing no harm. The concepts of justice, fidelity and trust are paramount, which is why our critique is to continually hold in mind the essence of embodying ethics, embodying professional values and embodying human rights and humanity.

4. Difference and diversity

In relation to difference and diversity, we acknowledge that the experiencing of trauma is idiosyncratic, meaning that we each experience it differently. Even if family members experience abuse within a similar context, the way that trauma affects each individual may be very different.

5. Learning from grandparents

It is important to note the transgenerational aspect of trauma and how trauma can form and develop over time. As practitioners, trainees and students grapple with the concept of trauma and how to work with/treat trauma, it is important to hold history in mind, and that an individual may come from a context where generations of their family may have been struggling with and trying to manage trauma.

6. Psychology of love

Our final point is that there is a concept that comes from the psychology of love: Robert Sternberg (Sternberg, 2006) presents the duplex theory of love, and says that everyone has a love story to tell. We are asserting that everyone has a trauma story to tell, whether that's a personal story or a transgenerational one. We are not pointing our fingers at others (such as Farrokh, Little V and Willow) and thinking that trauma happens to others. Instead, we are suggesting that this is part of the human condition that we all grapple with.

Demystifying trauma: final words

To conclude, we hope we have demonstrated how trauma can be complex and multi-faceted. At the same time, we can simplify the concept: we are social animals, and we have a history which is within us and a future which will be affected by experiences of the present. We can see the same thing in many areas of nature: in the sediments of rocks, in the growth of trees. We are part of nature and so we can come to describe trauma as a particular form of unpredictable shift in our being. While we have shared our understandings and experiences with you in this book, we encourage you to draw upon the Zen Buddhist concept of 'beginner's mind' to reflect upon the field at this current time and to continue to develop the way we understand and work with psychological trauma.

Reflection point 12.1

1 What are the advantages and disadvantages of the concept of post-traumatic growth, both for individuals and society?
2 Reflect on your thoughts about how our understanding and treatment of trauma might change moving forwards.
3 What are the key areas in the field of psychological trauma that you will explore further, having read this book?

Key resources and further reading

Chapter 2

van der Kolk, B. (2014). *The body keeps the score: Mind, brain and body in the transformation of trauma*. Penguin Books.

Love thy Neighbour (1972 TV-series). https://en.wikipedia.org/wiki/Love_Thy_Neighbour_(1972_TV_series)

BBC Radio 4 (2020). *The Life Scientific: Peter Fonagy on a Revolution in Healthcare.* Producer Anna Buckley. Broadcast 28 January. Available at: https://www.bbc.co.uk/programmes/m000dpj2 (via the BBC Sounds App).

Currier, J. (2022). Paper delivered to UKPTS Annual Conference, London, 2022 https://ukpts.org/2022/06/16/ukpts-2022-annual-conference-review/

The Healing Foundation, Australia (2011). Intergenerational Trauma Animation: https://youtu.be/vlqx8EYvRbQ?feature=shared

Chapter 3

Dana, D. (2021). *Anchored: How to befriend your nervous system using polyvagal theory*. Sounds True (Audio book).

Rothschild, B. (2000). *The body remembers continuing education test: The psychophysiology of trauma & trauma treatment*. WW Norton & Company.

van der Kolk, B. (2014). *The body keeps the score: Mind, brain and body in the transformation of trauma*. Penguin Books.

Chapter 4

Winter L. A., & Charura, D. (2023). *Handbook of social justice theory and practice in the psychological therapies: Power, politics and change*. Sage.

Chapter 5

Because of the fast-evolving nature of research in this area we encourage you to engage with the latest research within your modality or area of specialism.

Please see the following:

McFetridge, M., Hauenstein Swan, A., Heke, S., Karatzias, T., Greenberg, N., NHS Greater Glasgow & Clyde Board Members of the UK Psychological Trauma Society (UKPTS) (2017) Guidelines for the treatment and planning of services for complex post-traumatic stress disorder in adults. Accessed at https://ukpts.org/wp-content/uploads/2018/03/guidance_11_2920929231.pdf

We have also found the following webpages helpful as research is regularly reviewed and uploaded from a USA veterans context: Please see https://www.ptsd.va.gov/publications/ctu_online.asp

Chapter 6

Hipólito, J., Nunes, O., & Brites, R. (2014). Working with diagnosis within psychiatric settings: About diagnosis, evolution, and paradigm shift. In D. Charura, & S. Paul (Eds.), *The therapeutic relationship handbook: Theory and practice* (pp. 196–206). McGraw-Hill Education.

Johnstone, L., & Boyle, M. (2018). The power threat meaning framework: An alternative nondiagnostic conceptual system. *The Journal of Humanistic Psychology*, 2216781879328. https://doi.org/10.1177/0022167818793289

Sanders, P., & Tolan, J. (2023). *People not pathology*. PCCS Books.

Warner, M. S. (2013). Client processes at the difficult edge. In P. Pearce, & L. Sommerbeck (Eds.), *Person-centred practice at the difficult edge* (pp. 104–117). PCCS Books.

Chapter 7

Green, D., & Latchford, L. (2012). *Maximising the benefits of psychotherapy: A practice-based evidence approach*. John Wiley and Sons.

Natalia Nalyvaiko (2023). *Living in heroic trauma*. Testimonies from Ukraine 2023. Keynote paper at ESTSS 2023 Conference (Belfast). Available at: https://www.estss2023.com/keynote-speakers

Chapter 8

Australian Foundation for Indigenous sustainable health (2019). *Understanding intergenerational trauma* https://youtu.be/CvZEeXh1HdM?feature=shared

Herman, J. (1922/2022). *Trauma and recovery*. Pandora.

Pool, A. (1946). Physician superintendent's report for the year ended Dec 31 1946; The Retreat, York. Digitised records of the Retreat, York are provided by the Borthwick Institute, York *https://borthcat.york.ac.uk/index.php/ret*

The Retreat York, S Group (2011). Report on the meaning of spirituality. The Retreat, York. Digitised records of the Retreat, York are provided by the Borthwick Institute, York *https://borthcat.york.ac.uk/index.php/ret*

Stevenson, M. (1939). *Footsteps in the sand https://footprintssandpoem.com/mary-stevenson-version-of-footprints-in-the-sand/*

Chapter 9

Charura, D., & Paul, S. (2015). *Love and therapy*. Routledge. https://doi.org/10.4324/9780429476907

Gerhardt, S. (2015). *Why love matters: How affection shapes a baby's brain* (2nd ed.). Routledge.

Sternberg, R., & Sternberg, K. (2019). *The new psychology of love* (2nd ed.). Yale University Press.

Chapter 10

BBC Radio 4 (2020). *The Life Scientific: Peter Fonagy on a Revolution in Healthcare*. Producer Anna Buckley. Broadcast 28 January. Available at: https://www.bbc.co.uk/programmes/m000dpj2 (via the BBC Sounds App)

Herman, J. L. (2023). *Truth and repair: How trauma survivors envision justice*. Hachette UK.

Chapter 11

Charura, D., & Lago, C. (Eds.). (2021). *Black identities + white therapies*. PCCS Books.

McKenzie-Mavinga, I. (2009). *Black issues in the therapeutic process*. Palgrave.

Tudor, K. & Wyatt J. (Eds.). (2023) *Reflexive research for reflective practice: Qualitative research methodologies for psychotherapy* (pp. 72–86). Routledge.

Chapter 12

Jayawickreme, E., Infurna, F. J., Alajak, K., Blackie, L. E., Chopik, W. J., Chung, J. M., ... & Zonneveld, R. (2021). Post-traumatic growth as positive personality change: Challenges, opportunities, and recommendations. *Journal of Personality*, *89*(1), 145–165.

Kashyap, S., & Hussain, D. (2018). Cross-cultural challenges to the construct 'posttraumatic growth'. *Journal of Loss and Trauma*, *23*(1), 51–69. https://doi.org/10.1080/15325024.2017.1422234

Tedeschi, R. G., & Calhoun, L. G. (2004). Posttraumatic growth: Conceptual foundations and empirical evidence. *Psychological Inquiry*, *15*(1), 1–18.

References

Abrams, L. (2016). *Oral history theory* (2nd ed.). Routledge, Taylor & Francis Group. https://doi.org/10.4324/9780203849033

Adler, S. R., Fosket, J. R., Kagawa-Singer, M., McGraw, S. A., Wong-Kim, E., Gold, E., & Sternfeld, B. (2000). Conceptualizing menopause and midlife: Chinese American and Chinese women in the US. *Maturitas, 35*(1), 11–23.

Agyeman-Rawlings, N.K. (2018). *It takes a woman: A life shaped by heritage, leadership and the women who defined hope.* Hillcroft Bay Press.

Ali, D. A., Figley, C. R., Tedeschi, R. G., Galarneau, D., & Amara, S. (2023). Shared trauma, resilience, and growth: A roadmap toward transcultural conceptualization. *Psychological Trauma: Theory, Research, Practice, and Policy, 15*(1), 45–55. https://doi.org/10.1037/tra0001044

Allen, C., & McIntosh, V. (2023). *Child safeguarding and immersive technologies: An outline of the risks.* NSPCC.

Alleyne, A. (2004). The internal oppressor and black identity wounding. *Counselling and Psychotherapy Journal, 15*(10), 48–50.

Alleyne, A. (2011). Overcoming racism, discrimination and oppression in psychotherapy. In C. Lago (Ed.), *The handbook of transcultural counselling and psychotherapy* (pp. 117–129). Open University Press.

American Psychiatric Association. (2013). *Diagnostic and statistical manual of mental disorders* (5th ed.). American Psychiatric Association Publishing. https://doi.org/10.1176/appi.books.9780890425596

American Psychiatric Association. (2022). *The diagnostic and statistical manual DSM-5TR.* American Psychiatric Association Publishing.

An, S. Y., Kim, Y., Kwon, R., Lim, G., Choi, H. R., Namgoung, S., Jeon, S. W., Chang, Y., & Ryu, S. (2022). Depressive symptoms and suicidality by menopausal stages among middle-aged Korean women. *Epidemiology and Psychiatric Sciences, 31*, e60.

Antic, A. (2022). Introduction: Politicising children: Transcultural constructions of childhood and psychological trauma in the modern world. *Culture, Medicine and Psychiatry, 46*(3), 603–614. https://doi.org/10.1007/s11013-022-09805-1

Arizmendi, T. G. (2008). Nonverbal communication in the context of dissociative processes. *Psychoanalytic Psychology, 25*(3), 443–457. https://doi.org/10.1037/0736-9735.25.3.443

Asselbergs, J., van Bentum, J., Riper, H., Cuijpers, P., Holmes, E., & Sijbrandij, M. (2023). A systematic review and meta-analysis of the effect of cognitive interventions to prevent intrusive memories using the trauma film paradigm. *Journal of Psychiatric Research, 159*, 116–129. https://doi.org/10.1016/j.jpsychires.2023.01.028

Bailey, R. (2021). *Cingulate gyrus and the limbic system.* thoughtco.com/cingulate-gyrus-and-the-limbic-system-4078935

Bains, S. (2010). Racism as trauma: Reflective anti-racist practice in action (Chapter 3). In C. Lago, & B. Smith (Eds.), *Anti-discriminatory practice in counselling and psychotherapy* (2nd ed.) Sage.

Balkin, R. S., Lenz, A. S., Russo, G. M., Powell, B. W., & Gregory, H. M. (2022). Effectiveness of EMDR for decreasing symptoms of over-arousal: A meta-analysis. *Journal of Counseling & Development, 100*(2), 115–122. https://doi.org/10.1002/jcad.12418

Barthes, R. (1990). *A lover's discourse: Fragments*. Penguin Books.

Bateman, A. W., & Fonagy, P. (2004). Mentalization-based treatment of BPD. *Journal of Personality Disorders, 18*(1), 36–51. https://doi.org/10.1521/pedi.18.1.36.32772

Bateman, A. W., & Fonagy, P. (Eds.). (2019). *Handbook of mentalizing in mental health practice*. American Psychiatric Publishing.

Bateman, A., Fonagy, P., & American Psychiatric Association Publishing. (2019). *Handbook of mentalizing in mental health practice* (2nd ed.). American Psychiatric Association Publishing.

Bateman, A., Fonagy, P., Campbell, C., Luyten, P., & Debbané, M. (2023). *Cambridge guide to mentalization-based treatment (MBT)*. Cambridge University Press.

Beaudoin, M. (2005). Agency and choice in the face of trauma: A narrative therapy map. *Journal of Systemic Therapies, 24*(4), 32–50.

Beaudoin, M. (2022). Agency and choice in the face of trauma: A narrative therapy map. *Journal of Systemic Therapies, 41*(4), 67–85. https://doi.org/10.1521/jsyt.2022.41.4.67

Beck, C. T., & Watson, S. (2016). Posttraumatic growth after birth trauma: "I was broken, now I am unbreakable". *MCN: The American Journal of Maternal/Child Nursing, 41*(5), 264–271.

Bedard-Gilligan, M., Kaysen, D., Cordero, R. M., Huh, D., Walker, D., Kaiser-Schauer, E., Robjant, K., Saluskin, K., & Pearson, C. (2022). Adapting narrative exposure therapy with a tribal community: A community-based approach. *Journal of Clinical Psychology, 78*(11), 2087–2108. https://doi.org/10.1002/jclp.23395

Benda, R., & Pells, K. (2020). The state-as-parent: Reframing parent-child relations in Rwanda. *Families, Relationships and Societies, 9*(1), 41–57. https://doi.org/10.1332/204674319X15740695651861

Bion, W. (1962). *Learning from experience*. Karnac Books.

Bornioli, A. (2023). The walking meeting: opportunities for better health and sustainability in post-COVID-19 cities. *Cities & Health, 7*(4), 556–562. https://doi.org/10.1080/23748834.2022.2050103

Bornstein, M. H., Putnick, D. L., & Suwalsky, J. T. D. (2018). Parenting cognitions - parenting practices - child adjustment? The standard model. *Development and Psychopathology, 30*(2), 399–416. https://doi.org/10.1017/S0954579417000931

Bowlby, J. (1969). *Attachment and loss, Vol. 1: Attachment*. Basic Books.

Boyles, J. (2015). Working with refugees and asylum-seekers. *Therapy Today, 26*(8), 10.

Braga, L. L., Mello, M. F., & Fiks, J. P. (2012). Transgenerational transmission of trauma and resilience: A qualitative study with Brazilian offspring of Holocaust survivors. *BMC Psychiatry, 12*(1), 134. https://doi.org/10.1186/1471-244X-12-134

Brewin, C. R., & Burgess, N. (2014). Contextualisation in the revised dual representation theory of PTSD: A response to Pearson and colleagues. *Journal of Behavior Therapy and Experimental Psychiatry, 45*(1), 217–219. https://doi.org/10.1016/j.jbtep.2013.07.011

Brewin, C. R., Dalgleish, T., & Joseph, S. (1996). A dual representation theory of posttraumatic stress disorder. *Psychological Review, 103*(4), 670–686. https://doi.org/10.1037/0033-295X.103.4.670

Bronfenbrenner, U. (2000). Ecological systems theory. *Encyclopedia of Psychology, Vol. 3* (pp. 129–133). Oxford University Press. https://doi.org/10.1037/10518-046

Buber, M. (2008). *I and Thou*. Howard Books.

Butts, H. F. (2002). The black mask of humanity: Racial/ethnic discrimination and post-traumatic stress disorder. *The Journal of the American Academy of Psychiatry and the Law, 30*(3), 336. https://www.ncbi.nlm.nih.gov/pubmed/12380410

Bryant-Davis T., & Ocampo C. (2005). Racist incident–based trauma. *The Counseling Psychologist, 33*(4), 479–500. https://doi.org/10.1177/0011000005276465

Caizzi, C. (2012). Embodied trauma: Using the subsymbolic mode to access and change script protocol in traumatized adults. *Transactional Analysis Journal, 42*(3), 165–175. https://doi.org/10.1177/036215371204200302

Calhoun, L. G., Tedeschi, R. G., Fulmer, D., & Harlan, D. (2000). Parental bereavement, rumination, and posttraumatic growth. Paper presented at the Poster Session at the meeting of the American Psychological Association, Washington, DC.

Cappelli, F., Costantini, V., & Consoli, D. (2021). The trap of climate change-induced "natural" disasters and inequality. *Global Environmental Change, 70*, https://doi.org/102329. 10.1016/j.gloenvcha.2021.102329

Catherall, D. R. (2013). *Handbook of stress, trauma, and the family.* Taylor and Francis.

Cénat, J. M. (2023). Complex racial trauma: Evidence, theory, assessment, and treatment. *Perspectives on Psychological Science, 18*(3), 675–687. https://doi.org/10.1177/17456916221120428

Charura, D. (2024). Therapists' experience of working with refugees and asylum seekers who have been tortured: An interpretative phenomenological analysis. *Psychological Trauma: Theory, Research, Practice, and Policy.* Advance online publication. https://doi.org/10.1037/tra0001709

Charura, D., & Al-Murri, B. (2024). Racial trauma. In O. Nkansa-Dwamena, & Y. Ade Serrano (Eds.), *Race and counselling psychology.* Routledge.

Charura, D., & Bushell, S. (2023). A duoethnographic exploration of colonialism in the cultural layer of the objective psyche. *Journal of Analytical Psychology, 68*(1), 27–47. https://doi.org/10.1111/1468-5922.12878

Charura, D., & Clyburn, S. (2023). Critical race theory: A methodology for research in psychotherapy. In K. Tudor, & J. Wyatt (Eds.), *Reflexive research for reflective practice: Qualitative research methodologies for psychotherapy* (pp. 72–86). Routledge.

Charura, D., & Lago, C. (2021a). *Black identities and white therapies: Race, respect and diversity.* PCCS Books.

Charura, D., & Lago, C. (2021b). Towards a decolonised, psychotherapy: Research and practice. In D. Charura, & C. Lago (Eds.), *Black identities and white therapies: Race, respect and diversity.* (pp. 185–198). PCCS Books.

Charura, D., & Paul, S. (2015). *Love and therapy.* Routledge. https://doi.org/10.4324/9780429476907

Charura, D., & Smith, P. (2023). Post traumatic stress disorder. In T. Hanley, & L. A. Winter (Eds.), *The Sage handbook of counselling and psychotherapy* (pp. 300–307). Sage.

Charura, D., & Smith, P. (2024). A duoethnographic exploration of relational psychotraumatology: Research, training and practice considerations. *Counselling & Psychotherapy Research, 1.* https://doi.org/10.1002/capr.12749

Charura, D., & Wicaksono, R. (2023). Doing arts-based decolonising research. In S. Bager-Charleson, & A. McBeath (Eds.), *Supporting Research in counselling and psychotherapy: Qualitative, quantitative, and mixed methods research* (pp. 39–55). Palgrave Macmillan.

Chavez-Dueñas, N. Y., Adames, H. Y., Perez-Chavez, J. G., & Salas, S. P. (2019). Healing ethno-racial trauma in Latinx immigrant communities: Cultivating hope, resistance, and action. *The American Psychologist, 74*(1), 49–62. https://doi.org/10.1037/amp0000289

Chioneso, N. A., Hunter, C. D., Gobin, R. L., McNeil Smith, S., Mendenhall, R., & Neville, H. A. (2020). Community healing and resistance through storytelling: A framework to address racial trauma in Africana communities. *Journal of Black Psychology, 46*(2–3), 95–121. https://doi.org/10.1177/0095798420929468

Comas-Díaz, L. (2016). Racial trauma recovery: A race-informed therapeutic approach to racial wounds. In A. N. Alvarez, C. T. H. Liang & H. A. Neville (Eds.), *The cost of racism for people of color: Contextualizing experiences of discrimination* (pp. 249–272). American Psychological Association. https://doi.org/10.1037/14852-012

Connell, C. M., Pittenger, S. L., & Lang, J. M. (2018). Patterns of trauma exposure in childhood and adolescence and their associations with behavioral well-being. *Journal of Traumatic Stress, 31*(4), 518–528. https://doi.org/10.1002/jts.22315

Connolly, A. (2011). Healing the wounds of our fathers: Intergenerational trauma, memory, symbolization and narrative. *Journal of Analytical Psychology, 56*, 607-626. 10.1111/j.1468-5922.2011.01936.x

Cooper, M. (2023). *Psychology at the heart of social change.* Policy Press.

Cosgrove, L., & Shaughnessy, A. F. (2020). Mental health as a basic human right and the interference of commercialized science. *Health and Human Rights, 22*(1), 61–68. https://www.jstor.org/stable/26923474

Costa, P. T., & McCrae, R. R. (1992). Normal personality assessment in clinical practice: The NEO personality inventory. *Psychological Assessment, 4*(1), 5.

Cougle, J. R., Resnick, H., & Kilpatrick, D. G. (2013). Factors associated with chronicity in posttraumatic stress disorder: A prospective analysis of a national sample of women. *Psychological Trauma, 5*(1), 43–49. https://doi.org/10.1037/a0025954

Crenshaw, K. (1991). Mapping the margins: Intersectionality, identity politics, and violence against women of color. *Stanford Law Review, 43*(6), 1241.

Currier, J. (2022). Paper delivered to UKPTS Annual Conference, London, 2022 https://ukpts.org/2022/06/16/ukpts-2022-annual-conference-review/

Currier, J. M., Fox, J., Vieten, C., Pearce, M., & Oxhandler, H. K. (2023). Enhancing competencies for the ethical integration of religion and spirituality in psychological services. *Psychological Services, 20*(1), 40–50. https://doi.org/10.1037/ser0000678

Dana, D. (2018). *The polyvagal theory in therapy: Engaging the rhythm of regulation* (Norton series on interpersonal neurobiology). WW Norton & Company.

Dana, D. (2021). *Anchored: How to befriend your nervous system using polyvagal theory.* Sounds True.

Dashorst, P., Mooren, T. M., Kleber, R. J., de Jong, P. J., & Huntjens, R. J. C. (2019). Intergenerational consequences of the Holocaust on offspring mental health: A systematic review of associated factors and mechanisms. *European Journal of Psychotraumatology, 10*(1). https://doi.org/10.1080/20008198.2019.1654065

Deforges, C., Sandoz, V., Noël, Y., Avignon, V., Desseauve, D., Bourdin, J., Vial, Y., Ayers, S., Holmes, E. A., Epiney, M., & Horsch, A. (2023). Single-session visuospatial task procedure to prevent childbirth-related posttraumatic stress disorder: A multicentre double-blind randomised controlled trial. *Molecular Psychiatry*, https://doi.org/10.1038/s41380-023-02275-w

Deng, W., Hu, D., Xu, S., Liu, X., Zhao, J., Chen, Q., Liu, J., Zhang, Z., Jiang, W., Ma, L., Hong, X., Cheng, S., Liu, B., & Li, X. (2019). The efficacy of virtual reality exposure therapy for PTSD symptoms: A systematic review and meta-analysis. *Journal of Affective Disorders, 257*, 698-709. 10.1016/j.jad.2019.07.086

Diamond, G., Lipsitz, J., & Hoffman, Y. (2013). Nonpathological response to ongoing traumatic stress. *Peace and Conflict, 19*(2), 100–111. https://doi.org/10.1037/a0032486

Dias, B. G., & Ressler, K. J. (2014). Parental olfactory experience influences behavior and neural structure in subsequent generations. *Nature Neuroscience, 17*(1), 89–96. https://doi.org/10.1038/nn.3594

Dickens, C. (1857). *Little Dorrit* (1st ed.). Bradbury & Evans.

Dickens, C. (1868). *A Christmas carol. By Charles Dickens. As condensed by himself, for his readings. With an illustration by S. Eytinge, Jr.* Ticknor & Fields.

Duran, E. (2006). *Healing the soul wound: Counselling with American Indians and other native peoples.* Teachers College Press.

Dyer, K. F. W., & Corrigan, J. (2021). Psychological treatments for complex PTSD: A commentary on the clinical and empirical impasse dividing unimodal and phase-oriented therapy positions. *Psychological Trauma, 13*(8), 869–876. https://doi.org/10.1037/tra0001080

Effiong, J. E., Ibeagha, P. N., & Iorfa, S. K. (2022). Traumatic bonding in victims of intimate partner violence is intensified via empathy. *Journal of Social and Personal Relationships, 39*(12), 3619–3637. https://doi.org/10.1177/02654075221106237

Ehlers, A., & Clark, D. M. (2000). A cognitive model of posttraumatic stress disorder. *Behaviour Research and Therapy, 38*(4), 319–345.

Feltham, C., & Horton, I. (2000). *Handbook of Counselling and Psychotherapy.* Sage.

Ferentz, L. (2018). *Trauma informed assessments. A clinician's guide to safely identifying and exploring connections between clients' current struggles and prior histories of trauma, abuse, and neglect.* The Ferentz Institute: Advanced Psychotherapy Training and Education.

Fernández, V., Gausereide-Corral, M., Valiente, C., & Sánchez-Iglesias, I. (2023). Effectiveness of trauma-informed care interventions at the organizational level: A systematic review. *Psychological Services, 20*(4), 849–862. https://doi.org/10.1037/ser0000737

Finkelhor, D., Ormrod, R. K., & Turner, H. A. (2007). Poly-victimization: A neglected component in child victimization. *Child Abuse & Neglect.* 31(1), 7–26. https://doi.org/10.1016/j.chiabu.2006.06.008

Fonagy, P., Luyten, P., Allison, E., & Campbell, C. (2019). Mentalizing, epistemic trust and the phenomenology of psychotherapy. *Psychopathology, 52*(2), 94–103.

Forbes, D., Fletcher, S., Parslow, R., Phelps, A., O'Donnel, M., Bryant, R. A., McFarlane, A., Silove, D., & Creamer, M. (2012). Trauma at the hands of another: Longitudinal study of differences in the posttraumatic stress disorder symptom profile following interpersonal compared with noninterpersonal trauma. *The Journal of Clinical Psychiatry, 73*(3), 372–376. https://doi.org/10.4088/JCP.10m06640

Forster, J. (1876). *The Life of Charles Dickens: In two volumes. 1812-1847.* Chapman & Hall.

Foundation for Indigenous sustainable health. (2019). *Understanding intergenerational trauma https://youtu.be/CvZEeXh1HdM?feature=shared*

Frankfurt, S., & Frazier, P. (2016). A review of research on moral injury in combat veterans. *Military Psychology, 28*(5), 318–330. https://doi.org/10.1037/mil0000132

Freeman, D., Rosebrock, L., Waite, F., Loe, B. S., Kabir, T., Petit, A., Dudley, R., Chapman, K., Morrison, A., O'Regan, E., Aynsworth, C., Jones, J., Murphy, E., Powling, R., Peel, H., Walker, H., Byrne, R., Freeman, J., Rovira, A., . . . Lambe, S. (2023). Virtual reality (VR) therapy for patients with psychosis: Satisfaction and side effects. *Psychological Medicine, 53*(10), 4373–4384. https://doi.org/10.1017/S0033291722001167

Freud, S. (1900). *The Interpretation of Dreams: Sigmund Freud (1900).* Freud papers.

Freud, S. (1927). The question of lay analysis. In J. Strachey (Ed.), *The standard edition: The complete psychological works of Sigmund Freud, Vol XX (1925–1926): An autobiographical study of inhibitions, symptoms and anxiety. The question of lay analysis and other works* (pp. 1–292). Hogarth Press.

Freud, S. (1953). *Fragment of an analysis of a case of hysteria.* Hogarth Press.

Fromm, E. (1956). *The art of loving.* Harper.

Fuselier, G. D. (1999). Placing the Stockholm syndrome in perspective. *FBI L. Enforcement Bull., 68*, 22.

Gapp, K., Jawaid, A., Sarkies, P., Bohacek, J., Pelczar, P., Prados, J., Farinelli, L., Miska, E., & Mansuy, I. M. (2014). Implication of sperm RNAs in transgenerational inheritance of the effects of early trauma in mice. *Nature Neuroscience, 17*(5), 667–669. https://doi.org/10.1038/nn.3695

George, J. R., Michaels, T. I., Sevelius, J., & Williams, M. T. (2020). The psychedelic renaissance and the limitations of a white-dominant medical framework: A call for indigenous and ethnic minority inclusion. *Journal of Psychedelic Studies, 4*(1), 4–15.

Gerhardt, S. (2015). *Why love matters: How affection shapes a baby's brain* (2nd ed.). Routledge.

Gidycz, C. A. (2011). Sexual revictimization revisited. *Psychology of Women Quarterly, 35*(2), 355–361. https://doi.org/10.1177/0361684311404111

Giladi, L., & Bell, T. S. (2013). Protective factors for intergenerational transmission of trauma among second and third generation Holocaust survivors. *Psychological Trauma, 5*(4), 384–391. https://doi.org/10.1037/a0028455

Goldstein, J. L., & Godemont, M. M. L. (2003). The legend and lessons of Geel, Belgium: A 1500-year-old legend, a 21st century model. *Community Mental Health Journal, 39*(5), 441–458. https://doi.org/10.1023/A:1025813003347

González-Pardo, H., & Pérez Álvarez, M. (2013). Epigenetics and its implications for Psychology. *Psicothema, 25*(1), 3–12. https://doi.org/10.7334/psicothema2012.327

Graziano, R. C., LoSavio, S. T., White, M. A., Beckham, J. C., & Dillon, K. H. (2023). Examination of PTSD symptom networks over the course of cognitive processing therapy. *Psychological Trauma: Theory, Research, Practice, and Policy,* https://doi.org/10.1037/tra0001464

Grech, P., & Grech, R. (2020). A comparison of narrative exposure therapy and non-trauma-focused treatment in post-traumatic stress disorder: A systematic review and meta-analysis. *Issues in Mental Health Nursing, 41*(2), 91–101. https://doi.org/10.1080/01612840.2019.1650853

Green, D., & Latchford, G. (2012). *Maximising the benefits of psychotherapy: A practice-based evidence approach.* John Wiley & Sons, Ltd. https://doi.org/10.1002/9781119967590

Greene, T., Harju-Seppänen, J., Billings, J., Brewin, C. R., Murphy, D., & Bloomfield, M. A. (2023). Exposure to potentially morally injurious events in UK health and social care workers during COVID-19: Associations with PTSD and complex PTSD. *Psychological Trauma: Theory, Research, Practice, and Policy,* (Online ahead of print) https://doi.org/10.1037/tra0001519

Grzanka, P. R., Santos, C. E., & Moradi, B. (2017). Intersectionality Research in Counseling Psychology. *Journal of Counseling Psychology, 64*(5), 453–457. https://doi.org/10.1037/cou0000237

Gupta, N. (2022). Truth, freedom, love, hope, and power: An existential rights paradigm for anti-oppressive psychological praxis. *The Humanistic Psychologist, 50*(3), 460–475. https://doi.org/10.1037/hum0000274

Haigh, R. (2013). The quintessence of a therapeutic environment. *Therapeutic Communities: The International Journal of Therapeutic Communities, 34*(1), 6–15.

Haigh, R., & Pearce, S. (2017). *The theory and practice of democratic therapeutic community treatment.* Jessica Kingsley Publishers.

Hall, D. (2009). The middle passage as existential crucifixion. *Black Theology: An International Journal, 7*(1), 45-63. https://doi.org/10.1558/blth.v7i1.45

Harned, M. S. (2022). *Treating trauma in dialectical behavior therapy: The DBT prolonged exposure protocol (DBT PE).* Guilford Publications.

Hartmann, W. E., Wendt, D. C., Burrage, R. L., Pomerville, A., & Gone, J. P. (2019). American Indian historical trauma: Anticolonial prescriptions for healing, resilience, and survivance. *The American Psychologist, 74*(1), 6–19. https://doi.org/10.1037/amp0000326

Hauser, H. J. S. (2022). 'Pulling the bandage off': Using Margaret Warner's 'fragile process' in the psychodynamic approach. *British Journal of Psychotherapy, 38*(4), 693–708. https://doi.org/10.1111/bjp.12745

Heleniak, C., McLaughlin, K. A., Ormel, J., & Riese, H. (2016). Cardiovascular reactivity as a mechanism linking child trauma to adolescent psychopathology. *Biological Psychology, 120*, 108–119. https://doi.org/10.1016/j.biopsycho.2016.08.007

Herman, J. L. (1992/2022). *Trauma and recovery: The aftermath of violence – from domestic abuse to political terror.* Basic Books.

Herman, J. L. (2023). *Truth and repair: How trauma survivors envision justice.* Hachette UK.

Hinton, D. E., & Lewis-Fernández, R. (2011). The cross-cultural validity of posttraumatic stress disorder: Implications for DSM-5. *Depression and Anxiety, 28*(9), 783–801. https://doi.org/10.1002/da.20753

Hipólito, J., Nunes, O., & Brites, R. (2014). Working with diagnosis within psychiatric settings: about diagnosis, evolution, and paradigm shift. In D. Charura, & S. Paul (Eds.), *The Therapeutic relationship handbook: Theory and practice* (pp. 196–206). McGraw-Hill Education.

Hobfoll, S. E., Hall, B. J., Canetti-Nisim, D., Galea, S., Johnson, R. J., & Palmieri, P. A. (2007). Refining our understanding of traumatic growth in the face of terrorism: Moving from meaning cognitions to doing what is meaningful. *Applied Psychology, 56*(3), 345–366.

Holmes, S. C., Zare, M., Haeny, A. M., & Williams, M. T. (2024). Racial stress, racial trauma, and evidence-based strategies for coping and empowerment. *Annual Review of Clinical Psychology,* https://doi.org/10.1146/annurev-clinpsy-081122-020235

Huh, H. J., Kim, K. H., Lee, H., & Chae, J. (2017). The relationship between childhood trauma and the severity of adulthood depression and anxiety symptoms in a clinical sample: The mediating role of cognitive emotion regulation strategies. *Journal of Affective Disorders, 213*, 44–50. https://doi.org/10.1016/j.jad.2017.02.009

Jaffe, A. E., DiLillo, D., Gratz, K. L., & Messman-Moore, T. L. (2019). Risk for revictimization following interpersonal and noninterpersonal trauma: Clarifying the role of posttraumatic stress symptoms and trauma-related cognitions. *Journal of Traumatic Stress, 32*(1), 42–55. https://doi.org/10.1002/jts.22372

Jayawickreme, E., & Blackie, L. E. (2014). Post–traumatic growth as positive personality change: Evidence, controversies and future directions. *European Journal of Personality, 28*(4), 312–331.

Jayawickreme, E., Infurna, F. J., Alajak, K., Blackie, L. E., Chopik, W. J., Chung, J. M., Dorfman, A., Fleeson, W., Forgeard, M. J., & Frazier, P. (2021). Post-traumatic growth as positive personality change: Challenges, opportunities, and recommendations. *Journal of Personality, 89*(1), 145–165.

Jinkerson, J. D. (2016). Defining and assessing moral injury: A syndrome perspective. *Traumatology, 22*(2), 122.

Johnson, D. E., Miller, L. C., Iverson, S., Thomas, W., Franchino, B., Dole, K., Kiernan, M. T., Georgieff, M. K., & Hostetter, M. K. (1992). The health of children adopted from Romania. *Jama, 268*(24), 3446–3451.

Johnstone, L., & Boyle, M. (2018). The power threat meaning framework: An alternative nondiagnostic conceptual system. *Journal of Humanistic Psychology, 0*(0). https://doi.org/10.1177/0022167818793289

Johnstone, L. & Boyle, M. with Cromby, J., Dillon, J., Harper, D., Kinderman, P., Longden, E., Pilgrim, D., & Read, J. (2018). *The power threat meaning framework: Towards the identification of patterns in emotional distress, unusual experiences and troubled or troubling behaviour, as an alternative to functional psychiatric diagnosis.* British Psychological Society.

Joseph, S., & Linley, P. A. (2005). Positive adjustment to threatening events: An organismic valuing theory of growth through adversity. *Review of General Psychology, 9*(3), 262–280.

Joseph, S., & Linley, P. A. (2008). Psychological assessment of growth following adversity: A review. *Trauma, Recovery, and Growth: Positive Psychological Perspectives on Posttraumatic Stress,* 21–38.

Kanstrup, M., Singh, L., Göransson, K. E., Widoff, J., Taylor, R. S., Gamble, B., Iyadurai, L., Moulds, M. L., & Holmes, E. A. (2021). Reducing intrusive memories after trauma via a brief cognitive task intervention in the hospital emergency department: An exploratory pilot randomised controlled trial. *Translational Psychiatry, 11*(1), 30. https://doi.org/10.1038/s41398-020-01124-6

Kao, L. E., Peteet, J. R., & Cook, C. C. H. (2020). Spirituality and mental health. *Journal for the Study of Spirituality, 10*(1), 42–54. https://doi.org/10.1080/20440243.2020.1726 048

Kapend, R., Bijak, J., & Hinde, A. (2020). The Democratic Republic of the Congo armed conflict 1998–2004: Assessing excess mortality based on factual and counter-factual projection scenarios. *Quetelet Journal, 8*(1), 7–35. https://doi.org/10.14428/rqj2020.08.01.01

Kapoor, E., Okuno, M., Miller, V. M., Rocca, L. G., Rocca, W. A., Kling, J. M., Kuhle, C. L., Mara, K. C., Enders, F. T., & Faubion, S. S. (2021). Association of adverse childhood experiences with menopausal symptoms: Results from the data registry on experiences of aging, menopause and sexuality (DREAMS). *Maturitas, 143,* 209–215. https://doi.org/10.1016/j.maturitas.2020.10.006

Karatzias, T., & Cloitre, M. (2019). Treating adults with complex posttraumatic stress disorder using a modular approach to treatment: Rationale, evidence, and directions for future research. *Journal of Traumatic Stress, 32*(6), 870–876. https://doi.org/10.1002/jts.22457

Karatzias, T., Hyland, P., Bradley, A., Fyvie, C., Logan, K., Easton, P., Thomas, J., Philips, S., Bisson, J. I., Roberts, N. P., Cloitre, M., & Shevlin, M. (2019). Is self-compassion a worthwhile therapeutic target for ICD-11 complex PTSD (CPTSD)? *Behavioural and Cognitive Psychotherapy, 47*(3), 257–269. https://doi.org/10.1017/S1352465818000577

Kashyap, S., & Hussain, D. (2018). Cross-cultural challenges to the construct "Posttraumatic growth". *Journal of Loss and Trauma, 23*(1), 51–69. doi:10.1080/15325024.201 7.1422234

Katz, A. C., Norr, A. M., Buck, B., Fantelli, E., Edwards-Stewart, A., Koenen-Woods, P., & Andrasik, F. (2020). Changes in physiological reactivity in response to the trauma memory during prolonged exposure and virtual reality exposure therapy for posttraumatic stress disorder. *Psychological Trauma: Theory, Research, Practice, and Policy, 12*(7), 756–764. https://doi.org/10.1037/tra0000567

Keller, N. (2005). *The moderating effects of leadership, cohesion, and social support on the relationship between stress in combat, and the psychological well-being of soldiers participating in combat operations in Iraq.* Available from Sociological Abstracts: https://search.proquest.com/docview/61403058

Kira, I. A. (2001). Taxonomy of trauma and trauma assessment. *Traumatology, 7*(2), 73–86.

Kira, I. A. (2022). Taxonomy of stressors and traumas: An update of the development-based trauma framework (DBTF): A life-course perspective on stress and trauma. *Traumatology, 28*(1), 84.

Kirmayer, L. J., Gone, J. P., & Moses, J. (2014). Rethinking historical trauma. *Transcultural Psychiatry, 51*(3), 299–319. https://doi.org/10.1177/1363461514536358

Kisiel, C., Fehrenbach, T., Conradi, L., & Weil, L. (2021). *Trauma-informed assessment with children and adolescents: Strategies to support clinicians.* Concise Guides on Trauma Care Series. APA Books.

Kizilhan, J. I., Noll-Hussong, M., & Wenzel, T. (2021). Transgenerational transmission of trauma across three generations of Alevi Kurds. *International Journal of Environmental Research and Public Health, 19*(1), 81. https://doi.org/10.3390/ijerph19010081

Klest B (2012). Childhood trauma, poverty, and adult victimization. *Psychological Trauma: Theory, Research, Practice, and Policy, 4,* 245–251. https://doi.org/10.1037/a0024468

Knox, R., Murphy, D., Wiggins, S., & Cooper, M. (2013). *Relational depth.* Palgrave Macmillan.

Koebach, A., & Robjant, K. (2021). NETfacts: a community intervention integrating trauma treatment at the individual and collective level. *European Journal of Psychotraumatology, 12*(1), 1992962. https://doi.org/10.1080/20008198.2021.1992962

Kothgassner, O. D., Goreis, A., Kafka, J. X., Van Eickels, R. L., Plener, P. L., & Felnhofer, A. (2019). Virtual reality exposure therapy for posttraumatic stress disorder (PTSD): a meta-analysis. *European Journal of Psychotraumatology, 10*(1), 1654782. https://doi.org/10.1080/20008198.2019.1654782

Krediet, E., Bostoen, T., Breeksema, J., van Schagen, A., Passie, T., & Vermetten, E. (2020). Reviewing the potential of psychedelics for the treatment of PTSD. *International Journal of Neuropsychopharmacology, 23*(6), 385–400.

Krivzov, J., Baert, F., Meganck, R., & Cornelis, S. (2021). Interpersonal dynamics and therapeutic relationship in patients with functional somatic syndromes: A metasynthesis of case studies. *Journal of Counseling Psychology, 68*(5), 593–607. https://doi.org/10.1037/cou0000529

Kroener, J., Hack, L., Mayer, B., & Sosic-Vasic, Z. (2023). Imagery rescripting as a short intervention for symptoms associated with mental images in clinical disorders: A systematic review and meta-analysis. *Journal of Psychiatric Research, 166,* 49–60. https://doi.org/10.1016/j.jpsychires.2023.09.010

Kundu A. K. (2004). Charcot in medical eponyms. *The Journal of the Association of Physicians of India, 52,* 716–718.

Lago, C. (2006). *Race, culture, and counselling: The ongoing challenge* (2nd ed.). Open University Press.

Lago, C. (2010). On developing our empathic capacities to work inter-culturally and inter-ethnically: Attempting a map for personal and professional development. *Psychotherapy and Politics International, 8*(1), 73–85. https://doi.org/10.1002/ppi.213

Lago, C. (2011). *The handbook of transcultural counselling and psychotherapy.* McGraw-Hill Education.

Lago, C., & Charura, D. (2015). Working with transgenerational/intergenerational trauma: The implication of epigenetic considerations and transcultural perspectives in psychotherapy. *The Psychotherapist Issue 59- Spring 2015,* 23–25.

Lago, C., & Hirai, T. (2013). Counselling across difference and diversity. In M. Cooper, M. O'Hara, P. Schmid & A. C. Bohart (Eds.), *The handbook of person-centred therapy and counselling (*2nd ed.*)* (pp. 436–452). Palgrave MacMillan.

Lee, J. A. (1977). A typology of styles of loving. *Personality & Social Psychology Bulletin, 3*(2), 173–182. https://doi.org/10.1177/014616727700300204

Lely, J. C. G., Smid, G. E., Jongedijk, R. A., Knipscheer, J. W., & Kleber, R. J. (2019). The effectiveness of narrative exposure therapy: A review, meta-analysis and meta-regression analysis. *European Journal of Psychotraumatology, 10*(1) https://doi.org/10.1080/20008198.2018.1550344

Lensvelt-Mulders, G., van der Hart, O., van Ochten, J. M., van Son, M. J. M., Steele, K., & Breeman, L. (2008). Relations among peritraumatic dissociation and posttraumatic stress: A meta-analysis. *Clinical Psychology Review, 28*(7), 1138–1151. 10.1016/j.cpr.2008.03.006

Levi, O. (2020). The role of hope in psychodynamic therapy (PDT) for complex PTSD (C-PTSD). *Journal of Social Work Practice, 34*(3), 237–248. https://doi.org/10.1080/02650533.2019.1648246

Lewis, C., Roberts, N. P., Andrew, M., Starling, E., & Bisson, J. I. (2020). Psychological therapies for post-traumatic stress disorder in adults: Systematic review and meta-analysis. *European Journal of Psychotraumatology, 11*(1), 1–11. 1729633. https://doi.org/10.1080/20008198.2020.1729633

Linden, S. C., & Jones, E. (2013). German battle casualties: The treatment of functional somatic disorders during World War I. *Journal of the History of Medicine and Allied Sciences, 68*(4), 627–658.

Linehan, M. (1993). *Cognitive-behavioral treatment of borderline personality disorder.* Guilford Press.

Lingiardi, V., & MacWilliams, N. (2017). *Psychodynamic diagnostic manual* (2nd ed.). Guilford Press.

Litz, B. T., Stein, N., Delaney, E., Lebowitz, L., Nash, W. P., Silva, C., & Maguen, S. (2009). Moral injury and moral repair in war veterans: A preliminary model and intervention strategy. *Clinical Psychology Review, 29*(8), 695–706. https://doi.org/10.1016/j.cpr.2009.07.003

Livingston, N. A., Berke, D., Scholl, J., Ruben, M., & Shipherd, J. C. (2020). Addressing diversity in PTSD treatment: Clinical considerations and guidance for the treatment of PTSD in LGBTQ populations. *Current Treatment Options in Psychiatry, 7*, 53–69.

Lord, S. A. (2019). *Reflections on long-term relational psychotherapy and psychoanalysis.* Routledge. https://doi.org/10.4324/9780429054501

Maharaj, A. S., Bhatt, N. V., & Gentile, J. P. (2021). Bringing it in the room: Addressing the impact of racism on the therapeutic alliance. *Innovations in Clinical Neuroscience, 18*(7-9), 39–43. https://www.ncbi.nlm.nih.gov/pubmed/34980992

Manguen, S., & Norman, S. B. (2021). Moral injury. *PTSD Quarterly, 32*(5), 1–9.

Markin, R. D., & Coleman, M. N. (2023). Intersections of gendered racial trauma and childbirth trauma: Clinical interventions for Black women. *Psychotherapy (Chicago, Ill.), 60*(1), 27–38. https://doi.org/10.1037/pst0000403

Maslow, A. H. (1943). A theory of human motivation. *Psychological Review, 50*(4), 370–96.

McFetridge, M. A. (2001). *The process of EMDR therapy for post-traumatic stress.* Available from ProQuest Dissertations & Theses A&I: https://search.proquest.com/docview/301592831

McFetridge, M. A. (2019). Therapy beyond walls. *Clinical Psychology in the Mental Health Inpatient Setting* (pp. 17–30). Routledge. https://doi.org/10.4324/9780429464584-3

McFetridge, M. A., Milner, R., Gavin, V., & Levita, L. (2015). Borderline personality disorder: Patterns of self-harm, reported childhood trauma and clinical outcome. *BJPsych Open, 1*(1), 18–20. https://doi.org/10.1192/bjpo.bp.115.000117

McFetridge, M., & Coakes, J. (2010). The longer-term clinical outcomes of a DBT-informed residential therapeutic community: An evaluation and reunion. *Therapeutic Communities, 31*(4), 406–416. https://search.proquest.com/docview/875713217

McKenzie-Mavinga, I. (2009). *Black issues in the therapeutic process*. Palgrave.

McNeillie, N., & Rose, J. (2021). Vicarious trauma in therapists: A meta-ethnographic review. *Behavioural and Cognitive Psychotherapy, 49*(4), 426–440. https://doi.org/10.1017/S1352465820000776

Melby, M. K., Lock, M., & Kaufert, P. (2005). Culture and symptom reporting at menopause. *Human Reproduction Update, 11*(5), 495–512.

Metzger, I. W., Anderson, R. E., Are, F., & Ritchwood, T. (2021). Healing interpersonal and racial trauma: Integrating racial socialization into trauma-focused cognitive behavioral therapy for African American youth. *Child Maltreatment, 26*(1), 17–27. https://doi.org/10.1177/1077559520921457

Mikulincer, M., & Florian, V. (2000). Exploring individual differences in reactions to mortality salience. *Journal of Personality and Social Psychology, 79*(2), 260–273. https://doi.org/10.1037/0022-3514.79.2.260

Mikulincer, M., & Shaver, P. R. (2016). *Attachment in adulthood*. Guilford Press.

Miller, J.K. (2022). *The policing mind*. Policy Press. https://doi.org/10.2307/j.ctv2f1smgh

Miller, L., Bansal, R., Wickramaratne, P., Hao, X., Tenke, C. E., Weissman, M. M., & Peterson, B. S. (2014). Neuroanatomical correlates of religiosity and spirituality: A study in adults at high and low familial risk for depression. *JAMA Psychiatry (Chicago, Ill.), 71*(2), 1–8. https://doi.org/10.1001/jamapsychiatry.2013.3067

Mills, J. (2022). Treating a case of religious sex cult trauma. *Practice Innovations*, https://doi.org/10.1037/pri0000181

Moodley, R. (2009). Multi(ple) cultural voices speaking "outside the sentence" of counselling and psychotherapy. *Counselling Psychology Quarterly, 22*(3), 297–307. https://doi.org/10.1080/09515070903302364

Moodley, R., & Lubin, D. B. (2008). Developing your career to working with multicultural and diversity clients. In S. Palmer, & R. Bor (Eds.), *The practitioner's handbook*. Sage.

Moody, R. A. (2001). *Life after life*. Random House.

Morison, S. J., & Ellwood, A. (2000). Resiliency in the aftermath of deprivation: A second look at the development of Romanian orphanage children. *Merrill-Palmer Quarterly (1982-)*, 717–737.

Murphy, D., Elliott, R., & Carrick, L. (2019). Identifying and developing therapeutic principles for trauma-focused work in person-centred and emotion-focused therapies. *Counselling and Psychotherapy Research, 19*(4), 497–507. https://doi.org/10.1002/capr.12235

Nalyvaiko, N. (2023). Living in heroic trauma. Testimonies from Ukraine 2023. Keynote paper at ESTSS 2023 Conference (Belfast). Available at: https://www.estss2023.com/keynote-speakers

National Institute for Health and Care Excellence, (NICE). (2005). *Post-traumatic stress disorder: management. Clinical guideline [CG26]*. London, UK: National Institute for Health and Care Excellence; NICE. https://www.nice.org.uk/guidance/cg26

National Institute for Health and Care Excellence, (NICE). (2018). *Post-traumatic stress disorder: management. Clinical guideline [NG116]*. London, UK: National Institute for Health and Care Excellence; NICE. https://www.nice.org.uk/guidance/ng116/resources

Navarro, J. L., & Tudge, J. R. H. (2023). Technologizing Bronfenbrenner: Neo-ecological theory. *Current Psychology (New Brunswick, N.J.), 42*(22), 19338–19354. https://doi.org/10.1007/s12144-022-02738-3

Nikopaschos, F., Burrell, G., Clark, J., & Salgueiro, A. (2023). Trauma-informed care on mental health wards: The impact of power threat meaning framework team formulation and psychological stabilisation on self-harm and restrictive interventions. *Frontiers in Psychology, 14*. https://doi.org/10.3389/fpsyg.2023.1145100

Nwoye, A. (2017). The psychology and content of dreaming in Africa. *Journal of Black Psychology, 43*(1), 3–26.

Obermeyer, C. M. (2000). Menopause across cultures: A review of the evidence. *Menopause, 7*(3), 184–192.

O'Brien, C. V., & Charura, D. (2022). Refugees, asylum seekers, and practitioners' perspectives of embodied trauma: A comprehensive scoping review. *Psychological Trauma, 15* (7), 1115–1127. https://doi.org/10.1037/tra0001342

O'Brien, C., & Charura, D. (2023). Body mapping refugees and asylum seekers' perspectives of embodied trauma: An innovative method for psychotraumatology research & practice. *Qualitative Research in Psychology,* https://doi.org/10.1080/14780887.2023.2289964

Office for National Statistics (ONS) (2017) People who were abused as children are more likely to be abused as an adult: Exploring the impact of what can sometimes be hidden crimes. Assessed online. Available at https://www.ons.gov.uk/peoplepopulation-andcommunity/crimeandjustice/articles/peoplewhowereabusedaschildrenaremore likelytobeabusedasanadult/2017-09-27

Orlinsky, D. E., Grawe, K., & Parks, B. K. (1994). Process and outcome in psychotherapy: Noch einmal. In A. E. Bergin, & S. L. Garfield (Eds.), *Handbook of psychotherapy and behavior change* (pp. 270–376). John Wiley & Sons.

Oulanova, O., Hui, J., & Moodley, R. (2023). Engaging with minoritised and racialised communities 'inside the sentence'. In L. A. Winter, & D. Charura (Eds.), *Handbook of social justice theory and practice in the psychological therapies: Power, politics and change.* Sage.

Pals, J. L. (2006). Narrative identity processing of difficult life experiences: Pathways of personality development and positive self-transformation in adulthood. *Journal of Personality, 74*(4), 1079–1110.

Parnia, S., Spearpoint, K., & Fenwick, P. B. (2007). Near death experiences, cognitive function and psychological outcomes of surviving cardiac arrest. *Resuscitation, 74*(2), 215–221.

Patel, A. R., & Hall, B. J. (2021). Beyond the DSM-5 diagnoses: A cross-cultural approach to assessing trauma reactions. *Focus (American Psychiatric Publishing), 19*(2), 197–203. https://doi.org/10.1176/appi.focus.20200049

Patterson, C. H. (1974). *Relationship, counseling and psychotherapy.* Harper & Row.

Paul, S., & Charura, D. (2014). *An introduction to the therapeutic relationship in counselling and psychotherapy.* SAGE Publications, Limited. https://doi.org/10.4135/9781473909854

Paul, S., & Haugh, S. (2008). The relationship, not the therapy: What the research tells us. In S. Haugh, & S. Paul (Eds.), *The therapeutic relationship: Perspectives and themes* (pp. 9-22). PCCS Books

Pearce, S., & Pickard, H. (2013). How therapeutic communities work: Specific factors related to positive outcome. *International Journal of Social Psychiatry, 59*(7), 636–645.

Pedersen, D., Kienzler, H., & Gamarra, J. (2010). Llaki and Ñakary: Idioms of distress and suffering among the Highland Quechua in the Peruvian Andes. *Culture, Medicine and Psychiatry, 34*(2), 279–300. https://doi.org/10.1007/s11013-010-9173-z

Pells, K., Breed, A., Uwihoreye, C., Ndushabandi, E., Elliott, M., & Nzahabwanayo, S. (2022). 'No-one can tell a story better than the one who lived it': Reworking constructions of childhood and trauma through the arts in Rwanda. *Culture, Medicine and Psychiatry, 46*(3), 632–653. https://doi.org/10.1007/s11013-021-09760-3

Pierce, Z. P., Johnson, E. R., Kim, I. A., Lear, B. E., Mast, A. M., & Black, J. M. (2023). Therapeutic interventions impact brain function and promote post-traumatic growth in adults living with post-traumatic stress disorder: A systematic review and meta-analysis of functional magnetic resonance imaging studies. *Frontiers in Psychology, 14,* 1074972.

Pool, A (1946). Physician superintendent's report for the year ended Dec 31 1946; The Retreat York. Digitised records of the Retreat, York are provided by the Borthwick Institute, York *https://borthcat.york.ac.uk/index.php/ret*

Porges, S. W. (2017). *The pocket guide to the polyvagal theory: The transformative power of feeling safe.* WW Norton & Co.

Proctor, G. (2021). *The Dynamics of Power in Counselling and Psychotherapy* (2nd ed.). PCCS Books.

Read, J., Hammersley, P., & Rudegeair, T. (2007). Why, when and how to ask about childhood abuse. *Advances in Psychiatric Treatment: The Royal College of Psychiatrists' Journal of Continuing Professional Development, 13*(2), 101–110. https://doi.org/10.1192/apt.bp.106.002840

Reupert, A., Straussner, S. L., Weimand, B., & Maybery, D. (2022). It takes a village to raise a child: Understanding and expanding the concept of the 'village'. *Frontiers in Public Health, 10,* 756066. https://doi.org/10.3389/fpubh.2022.756066

Rivers, W. H. R. (1918). The repression of war experience. *Proceedings of the Royal Society of Medicine, 11* (Sect_Psych), 1–20.

Roberge, E. M., Weinstein, H. R., & Bryan, C. J. (2022). Predicting response to cognitive processing therapy: Does trauma history matter? *Psychological Trauma: Theory, Research, Practice, and Policy, 14*(5), 871–882. https://doi.org/10.1037/tra0000530

Rogers, C. R. (1959). A theory of therapy, personality and interpersonal relationships as developed in the client-centered framework. In S. Koch (Ed.), *Psychology: A study of a science. Vol. 3: Formulations of the person and the social context* (pp. 184–256). McGraw Hill. https://doi.org/10.1016/b978-0-08-017738-0.50039-9

Rogers, C. R. (1961). *On becoming a person.* Houghton Mifflin.

Rothschild, B. (2000). *The body remembers. The psychophysiology of trauma and trauma treatment.* W.W. Norton & Company.

Salem, M. O. (2006). Religion, spirituality and psychiatry. *Royal College of Psychiatrists SIG Newsletter, 21,* 1–15.

Sanders, P., & Tolan, J. (2023). *People not pathology.* PCCS Books.

Saul, J. (2022). *Collective trauma, collective healing.* Taylor & Francis. https://doi.org/10.4324/9781003231448

Scharf, M. (2007). Long-term effects of trauma: Psychosocial functioning of the second and third generation of Holocaust survivors. *Development and Psychopathology, 19*(2), 603–622. https://doi.org/10.1017/S0954579407070290

Schimmenti, A. (2018). The trauma factor: Examining the relationships among different types of trauma, dissociation, and psychopathology. *Journal of Trauma & Dissociation, 19*(5), 552–571. 10.1080/15299732.2017.1402400

Schmitt, S., Robjant, K., Elbert, T., Carleial, S., Hoeffler, A., Chibashimba, A., Hinkel, H., & Koebach, A. (2022). Breaking the cycles of violence with narrative exposure: Development and feasibility of NETfacts, a community-based intervention for populations living under continuous threat. *Plos One, 17*(12), e0275421. https://doi.org/10.1371/journal.pone.0275421

Schulenberg, K., Freeman, G., Li, L., & Barwulor, C. (2023). Creepy Towards My Avatar Body, Creepy Towards My Body. *Proceedings of the ACM on Human-Computer Interaction, 7*(CSCW2), 1-29. https://doi.org/10.1145/3610027

Shapiro, F. (1989). Efficacy of the Eye Movement Desensitization procedure in the treatment of traumatic memories. Journal of Traumatic Stress, 2(2), 199–223. https://psycnet.apa.org/doi/10.1002/jts.2490020207"https://doi.org/10.1002/jts.2490020207

Shapiro, F. (2018). *Eye movement desensitization and reprocessing (EDMR) therapy* (3rd ed.). Guilford Press.

Shay, J. (2014). Moral injury. *Psychoanalytic Psychology, 31*(2), 182–191. https://doi.org/10.1037/a0036090

Shuval, J. T. (1957). Some persistent effects of trauma: Five years after the Nazi concentration camps. *Social Problems, 5*(3), 230–243. https://doi.org/10.2307/798965

Siehl, S., Robjant, K., & Crombach, A. (2021). Systematic review and meta-analyses of the long-term efficacy of narrative exposure therapy for adults, children and perpetrators. *Psychotherapy Research, 31*(6), 695–710. https://doi.org/10.1080/10503307.2020.1847345

Sinalo, C. W. (2019). Decolonizing trauma therapy in Rwanda. In H. Grayson, & N. Hitchcott (Eds.), *Rwanda since 1994: Stories of change* (pp. 168–188). Liverpool University Press.

Smale, R., & Perry, J. (2003). 'Narrative as therapy'. *Person-Centred Practice, 11*(1).

Smith, P., & Charura, D. (2024). Working through relational trauma: An exploration of narratives of lived experiences of trauma and recovery. In Z. Boden-Stuart & M. Larkin (Eds.), *Relationships and mental health: Relational experience in distress and recovery*. Palgrave Macmillan

Smith, K. (2020). *Erich Fromm's 'The art of loving': An existential, psychodynamic, and theological critique* Available from ProQuest Dissertations & Theses: UK & Ireland: Business https://search.proquest.com/docview/2430703792

Smith, K., McLeod, J., Blunden, N., Cooper, M., Gabriel, L., Kupfer, C., McLeod, J., Murphie, M., Oddli, H. W., Thurston, M., & Winter, L. A. (2021). A pluralistic perspective on research in psychotherapy: Harnessing passion, difference and dialogue to promote justice and relevance. *Frontiers in Psychology, 12*, 742676. https://doi.org/10.3389/fpsyg.2021.742676

Sripada, R. K., Ready, D. J., Ganoczy, D., Astin, M. C., & Rauch, S. A. M. (2020). When to change the treatment plan: An analysis of diminishing returns in VA patients undergoing prolonged exposure and cognitive processing therapy. *Behavior Therapy, 51*(1), 85–98. https://doi.org/10.1016/j.beth.2019.05.003

Sternberg, R. J. (2006). A duplex theory of love. *The new psychology of love*, (pp.184–199). Yale University Press.

Sternberg, R., & Sternberg, K. (2019). *The new psychology of love* (2nd ed.). Yale University Press.

Stevenson, M. (1939). *Footsteps in the sand https://footprintssandpoem.com/mary-stevenson-version-of-footprints-in-the-sand/*

Stiles, B. W., Barkham, M., Clark, J. M., & Connell, J. (2008). Effectiveness of cognitive-behavioural person-centered and psychodynamic therapies in UK primary-care routine practice: Replication in a larger sample. *Psychological Medicine, 38*(5), 677–688. https://doi.org/10.1017/S0033291707001511

Straker, G. (1987). The continuous traumatic stress syndrome: The single therapeutic interview. *Psychology in Society, 8*, 48–79.

Straker, G. (1990). Long-term psychological stress as a traumatic syndrome – possibilities of a single therapeutic consultation. Sanctuaries Counseling Team. *Psyche (Stuttgart), 44*(2), 144–163. Retrieved from https://www.ncbi.nlm.nih.gov/pubmed/2315516

Summerfield, D. (2022). The politicised child, transcultural constructions of childhood, psychological trauma, and the mind in the modern world: Afterword. *Culture, Medicine and Psychiatry, 46*(3), 679–682. https://doi.org/10.1007/s11013-022-09804-2

Swanson, D. M. (2008). Ubuntu: An African contribution to (re)search for/with a 'humble togetherness'. *Journal of Contemporary Issues in Education, 2*(2). https://doi.org/10.20355/C5PP4X

Sweeney, A., Anenden, V., Bogart, K., Carr, S., Catty, J., Clement, S., Faulkner, A., Gibson, S., Gillard, S., Ion, M., Keeble, S., Kennedy, A., Kothari, G., & Samuels, L. (2021).

Evidence based guidelines for conducting trauma-informed talking therapy assessments. Online: Kings College London. https://www.kcl.ac.uk/ioppn/assets/trauma-informed-assessment-guidelines.pdf

Tan, L., Strudwick, J., Deady, M., Bryant, R., & Harvey, S. B. (2023). Mind–body exercise interventions for prevention of post-traumatic stress disorder in trauma-exposed populations: A systematic review and meta-analysis. *BMJ open, 13*(7), e064758. https://doi.org/10.1136/bmjopen-2022-064758

Taylor, M. (2014). *Trauma therapy and clinical practice: Neuroscience, gestalt and the body.* McGraw-Hill Education (UK).

Taylor, S., Charura, D., Williams, G., Shaw, M., Allan, J., Cohen, E., Meth, F., & O'Dwyer, L. (2020). Loss, grief, and growth: An interpretative phenomenological analysis of experiences of trauma in asylum seekers and refugees. *Traumatology.* https://doi.org/10.1037/trm0000250

Tedeschi, R. G., & Calhoun, L. G. (1996). The posttraumatic growth inventory: Measuring the positive legacy of trauma. *Journal of Traumatic Stress, 9*, 455–471.

Tedeschi, R. G., & Calhoun, L. G. (2004). Posttraumatic growth: Conceptual foundations and empirical evidence. *Psychological Inquiry, 15*(1), 1–18.

Terr, L. (1988). What happens to early memories of trauma? A study of twenty children under age five at the time of documented traumatic events. *Journal of the American Academy of Child & Adolescent Psychiatry, 27*(1), 96–104. *https://doi.org/10.1097/00004583-198801000-00015*

The Retreat York, S Group, (2011). Report on the meaning of spirituality. The Retreat York. Digitised records of the Retreat, York are provided by the Borthwick Institute, York https://borthcat.york.ac.uk/index.php/ret

Thielemann, J. F. B., Kasparik, B., Koenig, J., Unterhitzenberger, J., & Rosner, R. (2022). A systematic review and meta-analysis of trauma-focused cognitive behavioral therapy for children and adolescents. *Child Abuse & Neglect, 134.* https://doi.org/10.1016/j.chiabu.2022.105899

Thorne, B. (2012). *Counselling and spiritual accompaniment: Bridging faith and person-centred therapy.* John Wiley & Sons, Ltd. https://doi.org/10.1002/9781118329214

Tribe, R., & Charura, D. (2023). Counselling psychologists working in human rights & social justice. *Clinical Psychology Forum (Leicester, England: 2005), 1*(369), 37–46. https://doi.org/10.53841/bpscpf.2023.1.369.37

Tuke, S. (1813). *Description of the Retreat, an Institution near York for Insane Persons of the Society of Friends.*

UKPTS. (2022). *Moral Injury and Complex PTSD. https://ukpts.org/events/ukpts-annual-conference-2021-2022/*

Usall, J., Pinto-Meza, A., Fernández, A., Graaf, R. d., Demyttenaere, K., Alonso, J., Girolamo, G. d., Lepine, J. P., Kovess, V., & Haro, J. M. (2009). Suicide ideation across reproductive life cycle of women: Results from a European epidemiological study. *Journal of Affective Disorders, 116*(1), 144–147. https://doi.org/10.1016/j.jad.2008.12.006

van Assche, L., van de Ven, L., Vandenbulcke, M., & Luyten, P. (2020). Ghosts from the past? The association between childhood interpersonal trauma, attachment and anxiety and depression in late life. *Aging & Mental Health, 24*(6), 898–905. https://doi.org/10.1080/13607863.2019.1571017

van der Hart, O., van Ochten, J. M., van Son, M. J. M., Steele, K., & Lensvelt-Mulders, G. (2008). Relations among peritraumatic dissociation and posttraumatic stress: A critical review. *Journal of Trauma & Dissociation, 9*(4), 481–505. https://doi.org/10.1080/15299730802223362

van der Kolk, B. (2000). Posttraumatic stress disorder and the nature of trauma. *Dialogues in Clinical Neuroscience*, *2*(1), 7–22. https://doi.org/10.31887/DCNS.2000.2.1/bvdkolk

van der Kolk, B. (2014). *The body keeps the score.* Penguin Publishing Group.

van der Kolk, B. (2022). *How yoga helps with trauma.* YouTube. Retrieved 4 January 2024 from https://www.youtube.com/watch?v=TAGzGXBYBsI

van der Kolk, B. A. (1989). The compulsion to repeat the trauma: Re-enactment, revictimization, and masochism. *Psychiatric Clinics of North America*, *12*(2), 389–411. https://doi.org/10.1016/S0193-953X(18)30439-8

van Deurzen, E. (2015). Love and its shadows: An existential view. In D. Charura, & S. Paul (Eds.), *Love and therapy: In relationship* (pp. 13–24). Routledge.

Vecchio, E. A., Dickson, M., & Zhang, Y. (2022). Indigenous mental health and climate change: A systematic literature review. *The Journal of Climate Change and Health*, *6*, 100121. https://doi.org/10.1016/j.joclim.2022.100121

Vogt, K. S., & Norman, P. (2019). Is mentalization-based therapy effective in treating the symptoms of borderline personality disorder? A systematic review. *Psychology and Psychotherapy*, *92*(4), 441–464. https://doi.org/10.1111/papt.12194

Vontress, C. E., & Epp, L. R. (1997). Historical hostility in the African American client: Implications for counseling. *Journal of Multicultural Counseling and Development*, *25*(3), 170–184. https://doi.org/10.1002/j.2161-1912.1997.tb00327.x

Wagner, Z., Heft-Neal, S., Bhutta, Z. A., Black, R. E., Burke, M., & Bendavid, E. (2018). Armed conflict and child mortality in Africa: A geospatial analysis. *The Lancet (British Edition)*, *392*(10150), 857. https://doi.org/10.1016/S0140-6736(18)31437-5

Warner, M. S. (2000). Person-centered therapy at a difficult edge: A developmentally based model of fragile and dissociated process. In D. Mearns, & B. Thorne (Eds.), *Person-centred Therapy Today* (pp. 144–171). Sage.

Warner, M. S. (2013). Client processes at the difficult edge. In P. Pearce, & L. Sommerbeck (Eds.), *Person-Centred Practice at the Difficult Edge* (pp. 104–117). PCCS Books.

Watts, S., & Stenner, P. (2014). Definitions of love in a sample of British women: An empirical study using Q methodology. *British Journal of Social Psychology*, *53*(3), 557-572. https://doi.org/10.1111/bjso.12048

Weissman, D. G., & Mendes, W. B. (2021). Correlation of sympathetic and parasympathetic nervous system activity during rest and acute stress tasks. *International Journal of Psychophysiology*, *162*, 60–68. https://doi.org/10.1016/j.ijpsycho.2021.01.015

Williams, M. T., Heaney, A. M., & Holmes, S. C. (2021). Posttraumatic stress disorder and racial trauma. *PTSD Research Quarterly*, *32*(1), 1–9. https://www.ptsd.va.gov/publications/rq_docs/V32N1.pdf

Winnicott, D. W. (1960). *The theory of the parent-infant relationship. In the maturational processes and the facilitating environment.* International Universities Press.

Winter, L. A. (2019). Social justice and remembering 'the personal is political' in counselling and psychotherapy: So, what can therapists do? *Counselling and Psychotherapy Research*, *19*(3), 179–181. https://doi.org/10.1002/capr.12215

Winter, L., & Charura, D. (2023). *The handbook of social justice in psychological therapies: Power, politics, change.* Sage.

World Health Organization. (2022). *ICD-11: International classification of diseases* (11th revision). Retrieved 4 January 2024, from https://icd.who.int/

Wylie, L., Rita, V. M., Harder, H., Sukhera, J., Luc, C., Ganjavi, H., Elfakhani, M., & Wardrop, N. (2018). Assessing trauma in a transcultural context: Challenges in mental health care with immigrants and refugees. *Public Health Reviews*, *39*(1), 1–19. https://doi.org/10.1186/s40985-018-0102-y

Yehuda, R., & Lehrner, A. (2018). Intergenerational transmission of trauma effects: Putative role of epigenetic mechanisms. *World Psychiatry, 17*(3), 243–257.

Yunitri, N., Chu, H., Kang, X. L., Wiratama, B. S., Lee, T., Chang, L., Liu, D., Kustanti, C. Y., Chiang, K., Chen, R., Tseng, P., & Chou, K. (2023). Comparative effectiveness of psychotherapies in adults with posttraumatic stress disorder: A network meta-analysis of randomised controlled trials. *Psychological Medicine, 53*(13), 6376–6388. https://doi.org/10.1017/S0033291722003737

Zaccari, B., Higgins, M., Haywood, T. N., Patel, M., Emerson, D., Hubbard, K., Loftis, J. M., & Kelly, U. A. (2023). Yoga vs cognitive processing therapy for military sexual trauma-related posttraumatic stress disorder: A randomized clinical trial. *JAMA network open, 6*(12), e2344862. https://doi.org/10.1001/jamanetworkopen.2023.44862

Zhao, Z., Duek, O., Seidemann, R., Gordon, C., Walsh, C., Romaker, E., Koller, W. N., Horvath, M., Awasthi, J., Wang, Y., O'Brien, E., Fichtenholtz, H., Hampson, M., & Harpaz-Rotem, I. (2023). Amygdala downregulation training using fMRI neurofeedback in post-traumatic stress disorder: A randomized, double-blind trial. *Translational Psychiatry, 13*(1), 177. https://doi.org/10.1038/s41398-023-02467-6

Index

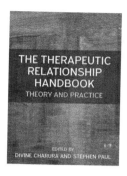

The Therapeutic Relationship Handbook:
Theory & Practice

Divine Charura, Stephen Paul

ISBN: 9780335264827 (Paperback)
eISBN: 9780335264834

2014

Practitioners across many counselling approaches acknowledge that the therapeutic relationship is central to therapy and its outcomes. This book argues that the therapeutic relationship cannot be reduced to particular words or therapeutic skills, but is a relationship encounter that promotes dialogue, contact and process. In each chapter, experts in different fields interpret the therapeutic relationship through the lens of their own modality, offering:

- Summaries of the key theoretical and research bases
- Example case studies of therapeutic interventions that illuminate key relational components of the approach and the development and management of the therapeutic relationship
- Study of the limitations, challenges and complexities of maintaining a therapeutic relationship
- Exploration of new developments in working with clients - capturing work that the authors and other colleagues have been involved in developing in that area

The Therapeutic Relationship Handbook is a broad ranging guide for students as well as both new and experienced practitioners.

www.mheducation.co.uk

The Person-Centred Counselling and
Psychotherapy Handbook: Origins,
Developments and Current Applications

Colin Lago, Divine Charura

ISBN: 9780335263547 (Paperback)
eISBN: 9780335263554

2016

From the origins of Carl Rogers' person-centred approach to the cutting-edge developments of therapy today, The Person-Centred Counselling and Psychotherapy Handbook charts the journey of an ambitious vision to its successful reality. In this book, Lago and Charura bring together history, theory, research and practice to deliver a complete and unique perspective on the person-centred approach.

Key topics include:

- **The groundbreaking journey of PCA's early decades, spearheaded by Carl Rogers**
- **Developments and extensions of the original theory and practice**
- **The influence of PCA in developing new therapies and practice**
- **The frontier of contemporary PCA, and therapists' work with client groups of difference and diversity**

With its broad view that explores the origins, variations and applications of PCA, The Person-Centred Counselling and Psychotherapy Handbook gives a comprehensive overview of the knowledge required and the issues faced by practitioners, making it an important resource for the seasoned and training practitioner alike.

OPEN UNIVERSITY PRESS
McGraw Hill

www.mheducation.co.uk

Trauma Therapy and Clinical Practice:
Considering Neuroscience, Gestalt and the Body

Miriam Taylor

2nd edition

ISBN: 9780335252473 (Paperback)
eISBN: 9780335252480

2024

Therapy with traumatised clients can be fraught with problems and therapists working with these clients seek greater understanding of the specific problems they encounter. Trauma Therapy and Clinical Practice weaves together neuroscience research and the experience of trauma, taking a fresh look at how original Gestalt theory informs our current understanding of trauma therapy.

The book:

- **Places trauma and trauma therapy in a relational field model** Includes material on change processes, triggers, dissociation, shame, enactment and resources
- **Describes clearly the neurobiology of trauma and the role of the body in maintaining trauma reactions and in the recovery process**
- **Offers experiments for deepening the therapist's embodied presence**
- **Provides numerous clinical examples and an extended case studies**

Miriam Taylor offers readers a theoretical basis for interventions and shows how simple Gestalt concepts can be applied in trauma therapy. By creating the conditions in which awareness, choice and vitality can grow, contemporary relational Gestalt is shown to be exceptionally well suited for trauma clients.

www.mheducation.co.uk

OPEN UNIVERSITY PRESS
McGraw Hill

Coaching and Trauma

Julia Vaughan Smith

ISBN: 9780335248421 (Paperback)
eISBN: 9780335248438

2019

Why do coaches need to understand trauma? This book highlights the role coaches must play – and how it differs to psychotherapists – in supporting clients with trauma. A role that both enhances the coach's skills and supports their clients' personal development.

Trauma isn't an event, it is a lasting internal process through which the 'here and now' of life experience is affected by the 'there and then' of traumatising experience. Vaughan Smith provides a way to understand the internal process that affects all aspects of our physical and mental wellbeing. While providing an introduction to the theory of trauma, the main focus is on practical application within the context of coaching; distilling Franz Ruppert's theory of the surviving self and the healthy self.

Written for practitioners, this important text raises trauma awareness, addresses the 'what if?' questions many coaches have and provides a clear framework for implementation. Rarely do coaching or organisational development books address the very prevalent issue of trauma and yet this is something every coach will come across in their practice.

www.mheducation.co.uk